ENDORSEMENTS

"Every now and then I meet a real 21st Century Marketplace Evangelist. Mike Moore is at the top of this list. He has probably shared Christ more effectively with high-powered people from all over the world from his living room than most Evangelist reach in a lifetime of crusades. Mike is a unique combination of intensity and freedom. A man of deep thought and equally deep feeling, you cannot meet him and not be impacted by the raw energy he radiates in his love for people. Mike deals in the real world of business and has a built in aversion to anything artificial. That is why he is the perfect person to write a book like this. I love him as a brother and respect him as a man, but I hold him in special regard as an ambassador of Christ in the marketplace. He is a true messenger of the gospel, in all its earthy essence. You will love this book, it is vintage Mike Moore."

Dr. Lance Wallnau

Lance Learning Group Dallas, Texas

"I met Mike in 1997. From the moment I met him, I knew he was different from anyone I had ever met. He had a light within him that was a mystery to me.

I was a workaholic and buried under the enormous responsibility of building Power House and directing the Dallas Mavericks Dancers. Mike gradually and steadily showed me Christ and the grace and freedom found in him. Coming to Christ transformed my life, and Mike made a huge impact on me as I was going through this process. His message helped me break the strongholds and chains I was living in by showing me true grace and freedom."

Shella Sattler
Choreographer for Michelle Obama's Let's Move Campaigns, Founder of the Power House of Dance

"Delightfully blunt, this book is an in-your-face challenge to consider the radical idea of liking God and believing He likes you too. Moore dares you to try enjoying faith instead of cowering in it. Whether you attend church regularly or get sweaty palms just thinking about it, this book will change the way you see Christianity."

Amy Spahn
Author of the Endurance series

Love God
Hate Church

♥ | ⛪

Love God Hate Church

MOVING PAST THE "DOS & DON'TS"

MIKE MOORE

For more information, visit:
www.mikemoore.co or www.lovegodhatechurch.net

Paperback: 978-0-692-58221-3
eBook: 978-0-692-58220-6

Library of Congress Control Number: 2015919197

*This book is dedicated to
my mom, Marie Moore,
whose last words to me were,
"Michael, **never** stop giving."*

Contents

FOREWORD BY BILL JOHNSON

My friend Mike Moore has the most unusual gift of hospitality I've ever seen. And that is saying something, since I live among champions in that area. In fact, we first met because of his kindness to me and my sons while we were visiting Texas for a few days. He left a permanent mark on my life.

Hospitality may seem insignificant to many—but not Mike's version. For him, it's a practical way of bringing the love of God found in Jesus into the day-to-day experiences of people he meets. Thousands of people have come face-to-face with the kindness of God in Mike's home—*tasting and seeing* that God really is good—all because he discovered a secret found in Genesis 28: *God's house is where God is.*

Does the title of this book offend you? I hope so. It offends me. And if you understand God's definition of the word, *church*, it probably does offend you. Of course Mike would never lift up his voice against what

God values, but since "church" has come to mean so many things other than what God intended, titles like the one of this book are useful.

Love God Hate Church is aimed at one deadly target: anything that claims to represent our heavenly Father but contradicts Him by actions, values, and controls that violate the nature of His heart. It's the same target that Jesus confronted, day in and day out, in dialogue with the Pharisees—that unseen element exalted by some that keeps a few people powerful while the rest grovel at the feet of those who rule. The leaders of these movements are the antithesis of the Father; they misrepresent the Kingdom of God completely.

I, too, hate these expressions that some mistakenly call "the church." They seem to declare that if we are good enough, keep the rules well enough, and follow their lead with enough focus and devotion, then perhaps we'll qualify for God's acceptance. That undermines the true gospel. But even then, we don't live in reaction to error. We live in response to truth—and more importantly, the One who is Truth.

Mike's passion for the authentic is visible in every part of his life. And perhaps that's why there was a cry in his heart to write such a book as this, so that people would take another look at the authentic.

I share Mike's passion for authenticity completely.

Here's a simple but profound truth found on these pages: *if you want to change your behavior, change what you believe. That's where it all starts. And if you want to change what you believe, start with God.* That is so powerful and true. Especially when one realizes that God is the perfect Father. All true knowledge starts with God Himself.

Mike Moore is a man who has experienced the freedom that comes from really knowing the heart and love of God as a Father. From that place, he longs to take the reader, and the countless visitors to his home, into the authentic expression of the gospel of Jesus Christ. Only this message—and this Father—can truly make one free.

- Bill Johnson
Pastor, Bethel Church, Redding, CA
Author of *When Heaven Invades Earth*

Introduction

My name's Mike Moore.

I love God.

I can't stand religion.

I don't hate the church in a literal sense. And I am differentiating between the institutional church and the body of Christ.

Jesus stated in Luke 14, "If anyone comes to me and doesn't hate his father, mother, brother, sister, wife, children, even his own life, he can't be my disciple." Jesus was speaking of priority, not to literally hate everyone and everything around you.

However, when any church anywhere puts rules, regulations, laws, terms, conditions, or restrictions before God's love, forgiveness, mercy, compassion, and grace, I think Jesus would say, "Go ahead and hate that church."

I'm really disappointed with the way the church tries to control not *what* we believe as much as *how* we believe and *why* we believe it. Can the church guide us? Sure—if it's not into modifying behaviors or managing its own image.

I didn't always believe this way. I was raised Catholic on the South Side of Chicago. As I matured and graduated college, there was a huge disconnect between how I thought God viewed me and the way He actually did. I thought that if I did all of the right things (attended church, didn't steal, didn't take another man's wife, didn't kill anyone, etc.), that I was doing OK. I read the Bible, taught classes on it, and even shared my beliefs with others. Yet, inside, I wasn't happy. I felt like God wanted more.

But I couldn't do any better. So I gave up.

I gave up until I realized that it wasn't God's fault if I viewed Him the way I did. What if the church got it all wrong? Or only half-right?!

If you feel the way I do about any of these topics, then maybe we should talk.

The problem with the world today is that if you want to get to God, you might think you have to go to a building, say this, do that, believe this, and don't believe that—or else God's gonna hate you, and you won't be accepted.

Are there sincere people in churches? Absolutely

there are, both in the pulpit and in the pews.

The problem is that the way the game is set up today, you have to go through rules and institutions if you want to get to God.

I say that's crazy.

God doesn't need you to make an appointment.

God'll see you right now!

God doesn't need you to come with someone else's opinion about how you should think, feel, believe, or not believe.

God is the ultimate come-as-you-are.

And why shouldn't He be that way?

After all, He created you just the way you are!

And He loves you just the way you are!

So this is a book for people who want to have a spiritual life but aren't all that crazy about what they've seen or experienced in some of our religious institutions.

Who am I?

Someone who's not too different from you.

Someone who's just trying to figure the whole thing out.

Someone invested in the process and not the outcome.

Why we're here. How we're supposed to be. And

what the deal is with God.

I'm not a religion guy.

Actually, I'm a businessman. I have a forty-year track record of success in the business world.

As a speaker, I've had the privilege of addressing audiences all over the world on the subject of spirituality, religion, and God. As a businessman. Not a cleric.

Jesus Christ's my guy. I dig Him.

I get Him.

And I hope to connect you with Him in a way that maybe you've never seen before.

This is a book of plain speaking, not empty philosophizing.

If you're sick and tired of being sick and tired, if you don't like other people defining your spirituality for you, and if you want to find a path to God that's truly your path, I might be able to help.

All I can say is, if you read these pages and you aren't shocked, outraged, moved, and called to a new love of God, then one of us failed.

Which one of us?

Mike

Part 1

UNLEARNING GOD

1

WHAT'S ON YOUR SLEEVE?

A few weeks ago, a friend of mine said to me, "You kinda wear God on your sleeve, Mike."

I thought that was pretty funny, so I said, "As opposed to what? What do you wear on *your* sleeve?"

He looked confused. "I'm not sure what you mean."

"I imagine you say that I wear God on my sleeve because I talk about Him all the time. So what do you talk about all the time? Whatever that is, that's what you wear on your sleeve."

My friend had no idea what he wore on his sleeve. Most of us don't. But believe me, we're all wearing *something* there.

Maybe you're always talking about how much money you make and your yachts and summer homes, or your fancy degrees and publication history, or how great and smart your kids are, or what a fantastic collection of clothes/art/stamps you have. Or maybe you take pride in your poverty. I think it's time we all became acutely aware of what we're wearing on our sleeves so that we can actually have a discussion about it.

When I said that to my friend, the conversation got real. I slowly began to realize that my God and the God he was seeing were two different Gods. The God he grew up with was not the same God I was talking about. And that made me sad—that my friend didn't know the God of my understanding, a God of infinite grace, love, and freedom.

"I've got news for you, my friend," I said. "Could be good news, could be bad news, depending on how you look at it. But here it is: You're going to have to unlearn God."

Most of us grew up with a God of rules and regulations, dos and don'ts. God was used as a stick—a punishing rod. "Do right, and God will bless you. Do wrong, and God will smite you down." So, basically, make good choices, and you get a reward; make bad choices, and you get punished.

That is not the God of the universe. God doesn't ever want us to confuse our behavior with His blessings. He's basically telling us, "Don't think of me as a vending machine—that you can press the button and there's your reward. You can make all kinds of mistakes, and I may still bless you. You can do something awesome, and not be blessed in the way you expected. I'm your God. I love you. I've taken away all your sin—that is why Jesus died for you. That's my gift. Now go enjoy life and love other people."

That's not the God many of us are familiar with. If that describes you, then you've got to unlearn the God you grew up with. It's imperative that you do.

In the groups I work with, I often ask people to describe the face of God. I say, "He's looking at you right now. What does His face look like?"

The responses I get are interesting. "Well, His eyes are really sad. Like He's a tad disappointed." That's the one I get most of the time—God is looking at them with vague disappointment.

"Okay, so He's a tad disappointed," I say. "Now if He were to say something to you right now, with that disappointed look, what words would come out of His mouth?"

Nine times out of ten, these people tell me God would say to them, "You can do just a little bit better."

That's most people's view of God: that He's a tad disappointed and thinks we can do just a little bit better. That's the God they grew up with. Meanwhile I'm sitting here going, "Are you kidding me? That is not the God that runs the universe!"

When I envision the face of God, He's got passion and fire in His eyes—and excitement! He sent Jesus to take away all our sins, and He's dying to be in relationship with us. He wants to pour His Holy Spirit on us to give us wisdom beyond our years. He wants to fill our heads and hearts with thoughts and feelings we would never have without Him, about how *He* sees us, not how other people see us or how we see ourselves. That's the God I'm talking about.

I don't follow a God who's only focused on rules and regulations for me to follow—who'll punish me or send me to hell if I don't do the right thing. My God isn't a giant cosmic killjoy. That's not why I get out of bed in the mornings. I get out of bed every day fired up with passion because my God is a life-giving God of passion. That's what He wants for me.

If I wear God on my sleeve, that's why. Because I'm excited about worshipping a God who fills me with His love, so I can go out and share it with everyone I meet. And so I can help people unlearn their God—and help them to meet mine.

What one thing do you need to unlearn about God?

2

FREE THE DAVID

On the South Side of Chicago, where I grew up, our whole neighborhood was Democratic. I was a Democrat, too. Do you know why? Because my mom and dad were Democrats. If you grew up on the South Side, you were a Democrat. That's just the way things were.

I grew up thinking Republicans were the enemy, simply because that's the way I was raised. But I didn't know *why* I believed that. I was just parroting what my parents said about politics.

It was the same with my belief system. I was a Catholic because I was raised that way. It's one thing for a kid to inherit someone else's beliefs, but for me, it didn't stop with childhood. Even as an adult, I was bound to this strict Roman Catholic way of thinking.

For years, I thought of God as "The Great Punisher," an arbiter who would judge me every time I screwed up. Why was I so quick to adopt everybody else's opinions, instead of taking the time to figure out what I believed?

As Socrates said, "The unexamined life is not worth living." And I agree: it's not.

Have you ever thought about how a sculptor creates a sculpture? Most of these guys have an idea in their head, and then they go get a block of marble. "Whatever I'm seeing in my head," they say, "I'm going to put it in this block of marble."

But Michelangelo said, "Not me." He would sit in a chair and look at a block of marble for weeks—sometimes even months—at a time, until he saw what was trapped *inside* the marble.

"Every block of stone has a statue inside it," said Michelangelo, "and it is the task of the sculptor to discover it." He chipped around and discovered the statue inside—and then he freed David from the block of stone.

The goal is to be freer at the end of this book than when we first started. That's the journey we're embarking on together: to bust free from that rigid block of stone. I want to free you with the thoughts and ideas I'm going to share with you in these pages. I want you to be free to unlock the treasure you have inside of you, so that people can meet the real you—not the imprisoned one who says, "Let's make sure we follow all the restrictions, rules and regulations, and commandments." Or, "Let's make sure we have all the right behaviors and look good doing it." I want your heart to desire a real relationship with God.

The idea of "freeing the David" inside of me was crucial in my own life. What did I need to chip away to free the real person who was inside me, the person *God* saw? My whole life, I'd felt like He was judging me for all the things I was doing or not doing, but what I didn't realize was that He had already judged Christ for every sin I ever committed. "I punished Christ for everything," God said. "And if I punished Him for everything, there's nothing left for you."

Only then did I begin to understand that my job was to receive that gift, get on with my life, and bring God's true love, mercy, and forgiveness to the world.

Are you ready free your David?

3

MEET MY SOURCE

Our view of God shapes who we are. The God I grew up with is not the God of my understanding now. Actually, it's more accurate to say that God hasn't changed, but my view of Him has changed.

If you and I are both at a museum, and we're looking at the same statue from different sides, we're not seeing it from the same perspective. I'm going, "Do you see what I'm seeing?" And you say, "No, I see something totally different." But the statue itself hasn't changed.

God allowed me to see Him the way He really is—a God of love and mercy, not a God who's here to judge us. When Jesus came to Earth, He didn't come to judge the world. He came to save us.

If you're in a lake, drowning because you can't

swim and bobbing up and down, and here comes a boat next to you and there's a guy inside, let me tell you what you don't need from that guy: swimming lessons! Can you imagine if, instead of throwing you a life vest, he said, "Now, here's what your problem is: you're splashing around too much and not keeping your head above water. I'm going to give you a quick swimming lesson. First, take your right arm ..."

You don't care. You're screaming, "Get me out of the water! I'm dying!" If he throws you a life vest, you're not going to care one bit about your form or your capacity as a swimmer. You're going to hold onto it with everything in you, because if that life vest doesn't hold you up, you die.

Jesus is the exact opposite of the guy in that boat. He didn't come to judge us; He is the life vest. He said it himself, "I came to save you."

After He saves us we are looking at Him and just being so grateful. Out of that gratefulness I start to wonder and ask why did you do this? And then I begin to discover that it is because of His great love for me. That's when my life begins to change.

Suddenly, I see evidence of God in everything around me—in the particles of the air, the sunshine, the chemical properties of photosynthesis... If you want to understand God, look at science. Look at astronomy. Look at quantum physics. Look at math. You study these fields and you go, "There's got to be a God behind this."

Let's say you have a very nice Rolex watch. It looks beautiful and it keeps time better than any watch you've ever owned. Well, who's behind it? A watch-maker. You can't get something as intricate as a watch without having a maker behind it. Just look at the universe! The sun has been in its place since the beginning of time, and it hasn't moved. Look at the stars—at Orion and all the other constellations and all the galaxies. It's absolutely amazing. So to say, "Well, I'm not sure there's a God." Are you kidding?

Let's go a little deeper. The diameter of the sun is approximately 865,000 miles. That's pretty large. In comparison, the diameter of the earth is approximately 8,000 miles. Wow. That's a big difference, right? The sun is over a hundred times larger than the earth.

Scientists call the distance between the earth and the sun an astronomical unit. One astronomical unit is 93 million miles. That's such a long way, scientists have to bring that number down so we can have a better mental understanding of the vastness of the universe. The nearest star (besides the sun) is 300,000 astro-nomical units from planet Earth. That is a distance of

93 million miles times 300,000. That's just incredible. Who are we dealing with here? The God of the universe who made this vast universe and put us on a tiny little planet called Earth!

Who is this God, and is He personal? Will He talk to us? Does He love us? Does He care about what we do and what we believe?

If God is managing a universe like the one we live in, do you really think He is looking at us going, "You know what? You're not pleasing to me. I don't like what you're doing."? No! He's offering us a gift of grace to bring us back in relationship with Him—and He's offering that gift of grace to everybody. How could we refuse that from the God who made everything?

When you realize how small we are in comparison to everything around us, God's offer becomes even more outstanding. What if God is saying, "You matter. You, individually, matter to me. I want to have a relationship with you because of what my Son did by giving His life for you."? That's the gift of grace!

That's pretty amazing. All of science should bring us closer to our maker, a God of love and mercy and a God of science. And yet for some reason we want to sit around with our fancy PhDs and intellects and discuss whether God exists! Come on. It's time we get real with ourselves, let alone with each other. Simply put, science is the study of the One who made it all—God!

There is a God of the universe. Believe this. Accept it. Let it change your thinking. Let that become the thought that changes your belief system and that will eventually change the way you look at other people and yourself.

Consider Jesus: He stepped out of time and space and became one of us, lived and died and rose again for us. And showed us that the God of the universe loves us with an unconditional love. No conditions. Come as you are. He said come AS YOU ARE.

Yes, we matter. What is keeping you from believing this and just coming as you are?

4

THE THREE VOICES

There are three voices in the universe today.

The first voice is the media: television, the Internet, social media, newspapers (if anyone still reads newspapers these days). Pick your poison. Whatever it is, we've got a steady IV drip of media voices screaming at us 24/7. Media is how people exchange and receive information. You turn on the TV, and it thinks for you. You lose three friends on Facebook and wonder, "What am I doing wrong?"

The media is the most pervasive of the three voices, because it's the one that speaks to us, relentlessly, every single day.

The second voice is the voice inside each of us, formed by how we were raised and what we believed. It's really a mash-up of hundreds of tiny voices—the parents, families, elders or teachers who started instilling their beliefs in us at a very early age. Whether they were Catholic nuns, Jewish rabbis, or Baptist preachers, the adults who instructed our young selves had a lasting impact on our future beliefs. We absorbed everything they did and said, forming that second voice—that voice in your head that says, "What would my mom think if I did this? What would my dad say? Will my friends judge me? How will people view me if I do this?"

Then there's the third voice. The third voice is the voice of God, and it's really the only one that matters.

Unfortunately, most people assume God's voice is judgmental and condemning. They picture Him as a heartless ruler with an iron fist, sitting up there on His throne, throwing down rules. People view God as a punisher, the sort of guy only interested in handing out guilty verdicts to His children. If you break a rule, you get struck by lightning. You got in that car wreck because you didn't obey Him. You didn't get that promotion because you broke Rule #3512b.

No wonder most people choose to listen to the first and second voices instead of the third! Even if the messages from those voices aren't always positive—we may feel judgment from our families, or we constantly get the message from the media that we'll never measure up—they somehow seem more relevant to our lives. And it's still better than listening to some vindictive God who's just setting us up to fail.

The irony is that God's voice is exactly the opposite of what most people think. It's the only voice in which there is the offer of *no* condemnation and *no* judgment—just compassion, mercy, grace, understanding, and forgiveness. That's the voice we need to wake up to every morning if we want to live happy, fulfilling lives.

But people are missing out on the one voice that truly matters. God's voice is the only voice that can get us through life, the only one of the three that can lead us to a place where we're genuinely happy, humble, and enjoyable to be around. God's voice guides and helps us, whereas the other two voices mostly bring us lies and harm, when they disagree with what God has already said.

Most of us ignore the third voice because we don't understand it. If I'm sitting at a Starbucks, and I really want to get to know a guy who comes in but he starts speaking Russian to me, I won't be able to understand him. He can talk all he wants, saying anything at all, but I still won't understand the language. He could even be telling me, "I'm about to kill you. I have a knife in my backpack, and I'm going to cut off your head," and I'd have no idea! I'd be laughing and smiling along with him, because I don't know what he's saying. He could also be telling me I'm the most incredible guy in the world and that he wants to put ten million dollars in my bank account immediately.

The point is this: I don't know what the guy's saying, so I'm probably not going to sit there and try to have a discussion with him. We wouldn't get very far.

It's no different with God. If we don't understand what He's saying, of course we don't want to listen to His voice! Everybody thinks God is all about what we do and don't do. They think He's all about behavior. But that's not who God is—that's only what people believe about Him.

The true voice of God is powerful—not because He's some taskmaster, but because He is a loving, forgiving, compassionate God. Compare that to the voice of the media, which says, "Buy this product if you want to feel worthy," or "If you want to be beautiful, you need to invest in this cream and that surgery." Compare it to the voice of some long-lost teacher or overbearing parent that tells you, "You'll never be good enough, no matter how hard you try."

What voice do *you* listen to? Which of these voices is predominant inside your head? If you're listening to the first or second voice, you're missing out on all the good stuff life has to offer. Once you hear the true voice of God in your head, you'll never want to hear another voice again. And the more you get used to hearing His voice, the more your voice to others is the same as His. That's what people really want to hear: when our words to each other become what God already has declared.

Get ready to be fully human!

What has to happen for you to hear His voice?

Most people think that going to church is the way we learn about God. And at times that's certainly true, if you're not being constantly told what to do and not do, but instead are being told how amazing God's love is for you. How passionate about you He really is! How ready He is to forgive and extend mercy and help!

We can also read His Word to us—the Scriptures. The book of promises to His kids. It's not a behavior modification manual; rather, it identifies our true nature as His children, and how His children receive and pour out His love to others.

Read it for ten minutes a day for one month. Believe it and trust it. Start in the Psalms, or Proverbs, or John. But just get started. Will you try it?

5

MIKE'S TEN COMMANDMENTS

Let's say you and your wife get an invitation in the mail. It's the fancy kind, with thick gold-leaf paper and a fancy red ribbon. You open the invitation and it says, "You are cordially invited to Mike Moore's house. Please come over whenever you'd like. Just let yourself in the front door."

"Well," you say to your wife, "Mike's a nice enough guy."

"*And* he has a pool," she adds.

You both agree: sure, why not? You'll come right over. But when you get to my house, you see a long piece of paper nailed to the front door. It's so long it's really more like a scroll. "**Mike's Ten Commandments,**" it says at the top, in bold black print.

MIKE'S TEN COMMANDMENTS

Commandment 1: You must leave your shoes at the front door before entering my house.

Commandment 2: You cannot, under any circumstances, use profanity in my house.

Commandment 3: There are three rooms you are not allowed in.

Commandment 4: You cannot go swimming unless you have a swimsuit on.

Commandment 5: You cannot touch the grill. That is my domain.

Commandment 6: You cannot walk into the wine cellar.

Commandment 7: You cannot use my washer and dryer. Only the housekeeper is allowed in the laundry room.

Commandment 8: Don't even think about touching the photographs on the mantle. To do so means you're lusting after the people in them.

Commandment 9: Do not eat the food in the fridge —any of it.

Commandment 10: Thou shalt not use more toilet paper than is absolutely necessary, at any time.

You think this is all a little strange, but you did both bring your swimsuits, and you're still hoping to take a dip in the pool. So, you enter the house warily. With each step, you feel increasingly anxious and uncomfortable.

Your wife starts to wander down the hall. "Wait, baby," you call out. "Hold on a second."

"What?" she says.

"Mike said we couldn't go near the wine cellar."

"He didn't say we couldn't go near it. He said we couldn't go *in* it."

"Yeah, but if we go near it, he'll think we're going to go in it. So maybe we shouldn't get within, like, ten feet of it."

Your whole conversation at my house has become about this: are you going to break the rules? You are not enjoying yourselves; you are worried and scared that you will mess up and be kicked out. Imagine how different it would be if I had stood at the door to greet you, saying, "Come on in, guys! How are you tonight? Good to see you! Let's go have some fun."

When I actually do have people over, I obviously don't have a list of rules posted on the front door. The whole reason I've invited you over is so you can enjoy yourself, and so I can get to know you better. Why? Because I want to relate to you. I don't need you to follow a bunch of rules in my house—that's not how we build a relationship.

Now, obviously, if you try to kill somebody under my roof, I am going to tell you that it's not appropriate. Certainly, there are *some* parameters I need you to abide by. My point is that the way God relates to us is no different than the way we relate to each other. He wants a relationship with you. He doesn't want you to tiptoe around following a bunch of arbitrary rules.

This is why I challenge people's views about God, because I want to help them unlearn all of the BS that has made them view God as a rule master. The God of my understanding isn't following you around with a grade book, marking a big red X every time you screw up and touch the grill.

If God's love for you is conditional—based on what you do or don't do—then the only thing you will focus on is the condition. You will not be able to have a relationship with Him. It's impossible. That's how it is with conditional love—it kills the potential for a real relationship because it becomes all about the rules.

Imagine a woman who says to her fiancé, "I'll love you no matter what, till death do us part. I'm in this relationship 100 percent, and I won't change my mind. But honey, there is one thing. If you burn the toast, I'm out. Other than that, I'll never leave you. You can embezzle money, or have an affair, or do anything else, and I'll still be right here by your side. But don't you ever burn the toast."

What is the one and only thing that woman's poor fiancé is going to think about? The toast!

"Oh my God, I can't burn the toast," he says. "As a matter of fact, I can't even have a toaster in the house. It's too risky. You know what? I won't even have bread in the house, because if the bread gets too close to a flame on the stove, it'll look like toast. So I have to make sure there's no bread."

So they get married, and he makes sure to have no bread products of any kind around the kitchen. But then one day his sister stops by with pastries, and he freaks out. "I can't have flour products in this house! What if the heat gets too high and they start to burn? Like toast?" He runs through the house in a panic, making sure the thermostat is under seventy degrees, and then he banishes his sister and makes her throw out all the pastries in the dumpster. He's completely lost his mind, all because of that one little condition.

The poor guy can't get past the toast. Soon it's all he thinks about. Eventually, the marriage fails because he is absolutely terrified of burning some toast-like object and his wife leaving him because of the ultimatum she gave him. Of course, in the end, she leaves him anyway.

Where is the intimacy in that relationship? It went

the way of the toaster: gone.

God's love is unconditional. He isn't holding a list of commandments over you with an ultimatum: follow all of these, and I'll love you, but break one, and I'll stop. "You're free to make a choice to do what you want," He says. "I will take away all your sins—past, present, and future—at the cross." And He says, "I will give you the gift of the Holy Spirit and the Holy Spirit will empower your life." We only have to humbly and freely accept what He's offered us. That's it. There are no other conditions between God and us.

That's the only way the human heart can be free— when there are no conditions in play. You can use my grill, go into my wine cellar, touch my photographs, and use as much toilet paper as you want, and I will not abandon you. In truth, I'll only love you all the more. You have to know that, no matter what you do, I will not abandon our friendship.

Remember the greatest need of the human heart is the forgiveness of sin. What is keeping you, right now, from fully receiving his love and forgiveness?

6

GOD GIVES A DAMN

The way we view God determines how we will live on planet Earth. Christian, atheist, Buddhist—doesn't matter. If you see God as a stern and strict father type, then you're not going to have very much fun believing in God.

One of my closest friends lost his dad six years ago. My friend was fifty-eight years old when his father got sick, and the two had never been particularly close. His dad had been pretty unemotional the whole time my friend was growing up—never the type to show affection or tell his son how much he loved him. As a result, my friend grew up with deep scars and spent most of his life self-protecting.

In the last months of his life, all his dad wanted to do was to sit in a chair and talk to his son. And finally, my friend agreed. So there the two of them were, in a hospital room together, at the bitter end. The old man tried to say all the things he wanted to say to his son, but my friend wouldn't let him.

"It's taken fifty-eight years for you to finally want to talk to me?" he said angrily. "When I was a kid, you wouldn't sit down and talk to me because it was all about you. And now you're telling me I have to sit down and hear whatever it is you have to say?"

Furious, my friend got up and walked out of the hospital. His father died that afternoon.

That just about broke my heart. And then I realized we do the same thing with God. We walk around going, "Yeah, God's out there somewhere, but He doesn't want to talk to me. He's not interested in me." And we miss out on these opportunities to let God speak to us—to hear what He has to say.

Why do we always assume God is this punitive judge, ready to slam down His gavel? We get in a car wreck or have a fight with our wife, and we assume God is punishing us. Really? Is that the way God is? What do you do when one of your kids disobeys you? Do you break both of their arms and put them in the hospital to teach the lesson? I hope not! That's not what loving fathers do—and God is the ultimate loving father. We tend to forget that.

All God wants is intimacy. *In-to-me-see.* He wants to look inside you and show you who you really are. He wants you to carry out His message to planet Earth: that He not only gives a damn about what He's created, but does it in a merciful, tender, compassionate way.

Every day, God is basically saying, "Son, sit on my lap. What's going on?"

To which you reply, "Well, Dad, you know what's going on. You're God."

To which He replies, "Of course I do, but I want you to tell me. I want to relate to you. I want to talk to you. Me and you. Let's just talk."

Here's the thing: God doesn't just love you, He *knows* you—intimately, inside and out. Even better, He's fully committed to you. Through God's love, you get to see what you're really like, and He likes you. He already knows what you're really like, because He made you in His image. Which is why that love will start to mold you into a compassionate, tender person, because that's who He is.

You know how we spend our whole lives trying not to turn into our parents, but we can't always help it? It's like that with God, too. Inside every human being ever to be born and live on planet Earth, there lives a desire to be exactly like the God of the universe. God put that desire in them.

Now, we can choose to say no. We can run from it. We can say, "Nah, I don't believe that." But why would we? God is the greatest role model you could ever have.

Maybe you didn't have good role models in your life. Maybe your parents set conditions on their love for you, and you felt that, no matter what you did, you could never measure up. Maybe your mom, dad, or some other adult in your life never cared about you one bit.

I'm here to tell you this: your Father in heaven is nothing like that. He gives more than a damn. He gave His one and only Son so that you could fulfill your purpose on this earth and have eternal life in heaven. Sit down in that chair right now and let him tell you so!

What do you feel Him saying to you right now?

If it's not uplifting, it's not His voice!

Part 11

CONNECTIVITY

7

HEY, GOD. WE HAVEN'T TALKED IN FOREVER

What would it be like to grab hold of God? To climb up onto His heavenly lap, pull His face down to our level, and tell Him about our day?

That's the kind of relationship He wants with us. Not this distant, cold, "Am I in trouble?" idea most of us have stuck in our heads. God wants to hold us and talk to us. And once we start grabbing hold of Him, we want to sit down with Him. We want to crawl onto the couch beside Him and say, "Hey, Dad—can I talk to you about something?"

A lot of us didn't have close relationships with our own dads, so it's hard to imagine crawling up beside a loving father. But that's what God wants. He craves it. Not only will He put down his paper and give us His complete and total focus—He will invite us to tell Him all about our day, because God is in the business of recognizing and validating us.

Now, I don't know what you've heard in the past about prayer or how you define it, but *that's* what prayer is. It's a discussion with someone who loves us. It really is that easy.

But somewhere along the way, prayer got "religiositized." I made up that word, but it fits the bill perfectly, because we've made praying seem so unattainable, so formal. Prayer was never supposed to be like that!

Prayer should be as simple as going to bed or getting up in the morning. That's infinitely better than a bunch of pre-set words you have to recite every night while kneeling on a cold, hard floor.

"The Lord is God in heaven and earth, and we all in agreement say, 'Amen!'" Say it enough times, and all the meaning is lost. That's not what prayer is. At least it's never what God intended.

Prayer is simply having a discussion with the creator of the universe. "Hey Daddy, I'm breathing air again today. Thanks for putting that air into the universe for me to enjoy. It's up to me what I do with that air. I know I could use it to fill up my lungs and then say a bunch of nasty curse words to my neighbor. Or I could use that same air to bless them. Thanks for giving me the opportunity, Lord, to bless people and not curse them. I like making people feel good about themselves."

Maybe you haven't prayed in a long time, and you feel nervous about it. Don't worry: God's not keeping track. You can start up again anytime, and He won't scold you. Maybe start with something along the lines of, "Hey, God. We haven't talked in forever. It's been twenty-two years since I've spoken to you, and first of all, thank you for not being like a human. If I didn't talk to a human for twenty-two years, we'd have to be in counseling for six months before we could even have that first conversation!"

In Luke 15:11-32, Jesus tells the parable of the prodigal son. The son has been gone for many years and has squandered his whole inheritance. In shame he returns home, and he has this whole rehearsed speech ready to give his father. "Dad, I screwed up. I wasted the fortune you gave me. I spent it on wine, women, and song, and I've been living with the pigs, eating what they eat. I've fallen so low, I'll happily be a servant in your house, if you'll just let me back in. I'm so hungry, but I don't deserve anything better than what the servants have." The son is so desperate that he'll take anything.

His father sees him coming from a distance and starts running toward him. He throws his arms around his son and kisses him. He puts his best robe on his son's shoulders and tells the servants, "Kill the best calf we have. We're having a party, because my son has come home." The son never gets to give his speech—his father won't hear it. In Dad's mind, there is nothing to apologize for. He is simply overjoyed that his son is home.

That's the God of the universe. He's not up there in heaven keeping score, giving us another demerit for every week or month or year that has passed since we've had a conversation with Him. He wants to talk to us. He invites us back to His heavenly table so we can have an honest-to-God heart-to-heart. He wants to kill the best calf and throw us a party, because He's so happy to be back in touch!

Do you believe it?

Do you believe that God is ready to talk to you?

WHO'S PROTECTING YOUR HOUSE?

A few years ago, I was convinced my house was impenetrable. I'd spent a good deal of time and money keeping my property and myself safe. When I was done, my house was extremely well fortified around the periphery. I had a tall, thick fence and double locks and bars on all the gates, and an airtight security system with a wire that would be tripped by an intruder. In case that wasn't enough, I'd put nails and sharp rocks on top of the fence, all the way around, so that no one could jump it. You'd essentially have to knock the whole fence down to get into my backyard.

I was mighty pleased with myself. I remember having a group of friends over and showing them the fence and the nails and the double-barred gates. "Nobody can break into this yard," I boasted. "I made it foolproof."

And wouldn't you know it—a few days later, I was out at a restaurant when I got a call from the alarm company.

"Mr. Moore? The alarm just went off in your house. Looks like it's the back bedroom window. Somebody's trying to get in."

I couldn't believe it. How had someone gotten through the fence and into the backyard? I hurried home, and, sure enough, the back bedroom window screen was bent. But the gates were still locked, and all the nails were intact! I couldn't make sense of it.

I started walking the perimeter of my property and stopped dead in my tracks. "Holy cow," I said. "You've got to be kidding me."

Somebody had bored a hole in my fence. Clean through it.

I called the police, and I was still standing there, staring at the hole, when they arrived. The officer came up beside me, scratched his chin, and said, "Why would they go through the fence and not over it?"

"You don't want to look up," I said.

He looked up at all the razor-sharp nails and rocks and laughed. "You're right. We didn't see that!"

"What would you do if a guy was trying to break into my yard and I shot and killed him?" I asked.

This was Texas, of course. The officer grinned and said, "Buy you a beer. You'd make our job a lot easier."

That night, as I was lying in bed, God spoke to me very clearly. "Who's protecting your house, Mike? Is it your nails and rocks, or is it me?"

I knew then I had to make a decision. God was right: I paid lip service to Him while bragging about how great my self-devised security system was. I gave talks about how we had to depend on God, to put our trust solely in Him, while I depended on my own strength and cleverness to protect myself.

Am I saying you shouldn't have a security system to protect your house? Of course not. Fortify your fences, guard your property, lock your doors. The problem was that I had stopped trusting in God to take care of me. I had begun trusting my own brains and brawn above the creator of the universe.

The Psalmist says, "Unless the Lord guards the city, the watchman stays awake in vain." Put another way, "Unless the Lord builds the house, those who labor, labor in vain." All my laboring to put nails on my fence and rig up a foolproof security system was in vain if I wasn't trusting Him.

So I talked with God that very night. "Wow, God," I said. "I'm sorry I've been trusting me."

What did God say? "Do what you gotta do, Mike. But look to me, because I am the One."

And He is.

He is the only one who sees us exactly the way we

are. The only one who sees our every motive. The only one who sees us when we believe our own BS.

And His response?

"I'm crazy about you!"

Seriously, are you as crazy about you as He is?

9

THE PRAYERS YOU HAVEN'T PRAYED

Praying is selfish.

It doesn't have to be, but for a lot of us, that's just the way it is. We pray when, and only when, we want something, clinging to the belief that God is a wish-fulfilling machine. Put a penny in, out pops an answer to a prayer.

Then, when a particular prayer doesn't come true, we turn our backs on God. "What a phony," we say. "He's not even listening."

But what do we pray? Even if our intentions are noble, our prayers still come from our own will and mindset. They come from our belief that the way *we* want things to be is the way they should be, and if God is really God, He'll make those things happen for us.

A lot of people mix God up with a religious system—a system that doesn't work—because their religion told them to pray, and then their prayers didn't have the outcomes they expected. Maybe, when you were a kid, you prayed for a pony and didn't get it. Or maybe you prayed for something more important, like for a sick friend or family member to get well. But when the result wasn't favorable—your friend or family member got much sicker, maybe even died—you grew angry and cynical.

"How am I supposed to deal with God," you say, "if He doesn't listen to me anyway?"

To which I say, "Oh, man. Are you ever human."

Before you ask yourself why God isn't answering your prayers, ask yourself, "What prayers *has* God been answering that I haven't even prayed?"

I'll give you one: the fact that you are breathing right now. Most people don't get up in the morning and say, "Lord, I want to keep breathing today. I want to live until the end of this day. Thank you for letting me come this far. I just want to give you thanks." I don't know about you, but I don't know many people who pray that prayer. And yet, if you're reading this book, it is safe to assume God has answered this un-prayed prayer for you today. God kept you alive. God let you live to see another day. He put air in the earth's atmosphere and lungs in your chest so that you could breathe.

There is so much in this universe we take for granted—the oxygen we breathe in, the carbon dioxide we breathe out. Guess what? God is behind that whole process! He exhaled once and said, "That should last for thousands of years. Breathe off that." And we did.

Next time you find yourself thinking, "God doesn't answer my prayers," I want you to think about the prayers you haven't prayed. Think about everything He does that you're not even asking Him to. If you were to make a list of those prayers, you'd probably be writing nonstop for a week.

Why do we continue to focus on the one prayer we did pray that didn't get answered, rather than the literally thousands of prayers we didn't pray that did?

The relationship we have with God is just that: a relationship. And when it comes to having our prayers answered, God is like a parent, and you're the little kid.

Let's say you're four years old and you turn five in January. So you go up to your dad and say, "Daddy, can I have a bicycle for my birthday? I want one of the shiny new red ones." You plead with your mom and dad for hours. You're praying, absolutely begging them to get you a bike.

The only problem is you don't actually know how to ride a bike yet. And your parents know that—they know you're not ready—so they don't get you a bike for your birthday. They want you to get some practice time on your big sister's tricycle first. They're trying to keep you safe, and they also want to make sure you're ready and prepared to own your very own bike.

But you don't understand that, because you are four years old, and you only see the immediate reality right in front of you. And in that immediate reality, all you want is a bike, and your parents are mean for not giving it to you. You spend months and months whining and pouting, asking yourself why your parents don't listen to you, why they don't love you.

Fast-forward eleven months, and wouldn't you know it; there's a shiny red bicycle underneath the Christmas tree with a big red bow on it. It's for you. Your parents love you more than you can imagine. They were just waiting for the right time to give you the very thing you wanted, knowing their timing is infinitely better than yours.

That's how it is with God. He loves us more than we can imagine. But we can't pretend to know His timing—we're basically overgrown kids in a big, scary, uncertain world. If it weren't for God looking out for us, we'd get squashed on the asphalt in a heartbeat.

There's one thing we can know for sure: His timing is better than our timing. The more we can trust that, the more prayer becomes an enjoyable conversation with our Creator, rather than a tally system in which we're keeping track of all the ways God let us down.

Next time you find yourself thinking, "Why doesn't God answer my prayers?" I want you to think about all the prayers He *has* answered. The prayers you may have never prayed.

Take just five minutes now, right now. Think about some things that have happened to you that you never asked for, positive things—an iPhone, technology, the ability to read and write. Before you dismiss this, saying that everyone has these things, remember there are seven billion people on planet Earth. If you live in America, you are in the top 5 to 10 percent of the world's population in wealth.

God, thanks for answering my un-prayed prayers!

Are you willing to thank God for all the things you never asked for that you have received, or will you focus only on the few things you asked for that you haven't received?

10

I'M ALL IN

I like watching poker on ESPN. These guys are playing Texas Hold 'Em. When you watch them on TV, you see how they look at their hands, and when they place a bet—whether they're bluffing or they've actually got a good hand— inevitably, one guy goes, "I'm all in."

Of course they've all got stacks of chips—fifty grand, one hundred grand, whatever it is. "I'm all in," says the poker player. Basically he's saying, "Since I'm all in, this is my last hand. Either I win or I lose. I'm putting it all on the table."

I love that picture. That's what God did when He chose us. He said, "I'm all in. It's not about you. It's about me. I put it all on the line. I sent my son. I did what I did. And I'm offering you the gift of grace."

God does not guarantee that you're going to

accept that gift. Millions of people don't.

But that doesn't matter to God. He says, "I'm all in. And my gamble is that my love, my grace, and my mercy are going to radically transform your life," if you receive it.

God doesn't need glasses. He says, "I'm betting my view will change who you think you are, and it will change how you deal with yourselves and others." And He's exactly right.

There's a book by Bill Thrall called *TrueFaced*. Bill talks about something called "The New Covenant Gamble." I don't usually quote from other books, but this one's too good not to. Listen to God's heart— the God of the universe:

> *What if I tell them, us, His people, there are no lists to follow? What if I tell them I don't keep a log of past offenses or how little they pray, how often they've let me down, made promises that they don't keep? What if I tell them they are righteous with my righteousness? They can do no wrong right now. What if I tell them they can stop beating themselves up? That they can stop being so formal, stiff, and jumpy around me?*
>
> *What if I tell them I'm crazy about them? What if I tell them even if they run to the ends of*

the Earth and do the most horrible, unthinkable things, that when they come back, I'd receive them with tears and a party? What if I tell them that I'm their Savior? They're going to heaven no matter what. It's a done deal. What if I tell them they have a new nature? Saints. Not saved sinners who should now buck up and be better Christians. After all, look what I've done for you.

What if I tell them I actually live in them now, that I've put my love, power, and nature inside of them at their disposal? What if I tell them they don't have to put on a mask? That it's okay to be who they are at this moment with all their junk? That they don't need to pretend about how close we are, how much they pray or don't pray, how much Bible they read or don't?

What if they knew they don't have to look over their shoulder for fear if things get too good, the other shoe's going to drop? What if they knew I will never ever use the word "punish" in relation to them? What if they knew that when they mess up, I will never get back at them? What if they were convinced that bad circumstances aren't my way of evening the score for taking advantage of me? What if they knew the basis of our friendship isn't how little they sin, but how much they let me love them? What *if I tell them they can hurt my heart, but that I will never hurt theirs?*

What if I tell them I like Eric Clapton's music, too? What if I tell them I never really liked the Christmas hand bell deal with the white gloves at church? What if I tell them they can be open with their eyes when they pray and still go to heaven? What if I tell them there's no secret agenda, no trap door? What if I tell them it isn't about their self-effort but allowing me to live my life through them?

I love that. And what if that were true? How would that change the way we live our lives? That's faith. That's the God I'm talking about. It really is a love story—a love story in which God loves and chooses and pursues us, His children.

To hear that is one thing. To really understand it, to believe it, and to absorb it into our hearts and our beings is harder. It requires us to have tremendous hope.

What is "hope" really? Hope is the confident expectation of good. But we use the word so much in our daily lives, we've stripped it of its meaning. We say, "I hope it rains tomorrow." "I hope I get a job." "I hope I get married someday." "I hope I live to be ninety."

That's not the hope I'm talking about. The hope

I'm talking about is a confident expectation that good will happen. That is the hope in the God of the universe. That's the God I'm talking about. When we put our hope in Him, we have a confident expectation that good is going to occur, and it will. Why? Because God is all in.

And He will never change His mind on that.

Are you all in?

Part III

INTRODUCING THE PLAINTIFF

11

MEET THE ADVERSARY

There's an old joke about the Fall of Man.

What excuse did Adam give to his children as to why he no longer lived in Eden?

"Well, kids, your mother ate us out of house and home."

It's a funny gag, but I often feel genuine sympathy for Eve. Eve was created *after* God commanded Adam to not eat from the tree of the knowledge of good and evil. So she heard the command from her husband, not from God Himself. This left her particularly susceptible when the enemy came and twisted the truth. "Did God say you couldn't eat from any tree here in the garden?" Satan said.

"No, no, no," Eve replied. "God just said we couldn't eat from *that* tree ..."

The battle was already lost, because now Eve was in conversation with the enemy. Satan was another voice in the universe. Before he slithered onto the scene in the form of a serpent, it was only God speaking to Adam and Eve.

The serpent was brilliantly manipulative. Once he had engaged Eve, he started messing with her, twisting God's commandment around until it was mangled in her mind. Eve took the fruit and ate it. At first everything seemed fine. So she gave it to Adam, who also ate of the fruit.

And then suddenly they both realized they were naked. They hid themselves from God, but He found them, because He's God. And Adam said, "I hid because I was naked," to which God replied, "Who told you that you were naked?"

For all you vegetarians out there, I hate to say it, but this was when God killed the first animal. He clothed Adam and Eve in the skins. This was the first blood sacrifice for sin.

Up to that point, Adam had total authority over planet Earth. But in that moment of eating the fruit from the tree of the knowledge of good and evil, Adam took that authority and handed it over to Satan.

Many years later, the Messiah would come and

take it back.

Christ came to Earth not as a conquering king, but as a servant. He was born of a virgin and worked as a carpenter. Only a being that was 100 percent man and 100 percent God could take the reins back from the enemy. The first man, Adam, did not obey God completely. But Jesus, God's son, did.

Once you understand that you are living in a world of good and evil, you get to make a choice. All you have to do is turn on the news to see that bad things happen to good people. Children get sick and accidents happen. It's part of life. But I like to hold onto Psalm 91:7-10:

> *A thousand may fall at your side*
> *And ten thousand at your right hand,*
> *But it shall not approach you.*
> *You will only look on with your eyes*
> *And see the recompense of the wicked.*
> *For you have made the Lord, my refuge,*
> *Even the Most High, your dwelling place.*
> *No evil will befall you,*
> *Nor will any plague come near your dwelling.*

That's a covenant that God made with His people. I either believe that or I don't.

Until the day when God decisively ends Satan's influence, we are all in a battle with the enemy and his spiritual forces. But God has given us the tools we need to wage war—and emerge triumphant.

These tools include believing what God has written in his Word and believing that we have the promised Holy Spirit, and then we can vanquish all the evil that ever comes our way. All we have to hold on to are the promises in His Word. This is why Scripture is the most important document on the planet. It's instructions from a heavenly father to a people whom He loves. Whether you're a believer or not, that is a beautiful thing.

Which voice are you listening to?

12

CASE DISMISSED

Picture me, Mike Moore, standing in a courtroom. God the father is the judge, and Satan, the enemy, is the prosecuting attorney.

I'm standing before God when Satan comes in, all cool and slick, so charming you might not even know he's pure evil under that pinstriped Armani suit. "Ladies and gentlemen of the jury," he says, "I'm here today to do one thing. I'm here to expose this scumbag standing before you."

My heart sinks. Every fiber of my being knows I'm the scumbag he's referring to.

"This is going to be pretty easy for me," Satan goes on, "because I'm going off the law the Father wrote. I didn't write it—it wasn't my idea. I'm just a humble attorney. So all I'm going to do is examine this scumbag's life, and hold it up to the law. From the beginning to the end of Mike's life, every time there was some discrepancy with God's law, every time he screwed up, I've jotted it down on a pad of paper." He holds up a bright yellow legal pad. "Like this one here.

"So, ladies and gentlemen of the jury," he says with a dramatic flourish, "take this as exhibit one."

And wouldn't you know it—suddenly a forty-foot tractor-trailer is steamrolling into the courtroom. It's filled from top to bottom with yellow legal pads chronicling every time I made a mistake, or will make a mistake, against God's law: every lie, sin, angry word, and lustful thought. All the sins of my entire life are right there on paper.

"So, ladies and gentlemen of the jury," Satan says, "as you can see, this guy deserves life in prison or the death penalty. I rest my case."

The father, God the judge, looks down at me from His seat. "Where is your representation, son?" He says, not unkindly. "Your attorney?"

"Uh, I don't know. He's a little late, maybe."

Then all of a sudden, the doors to the courtroom bust open, and my attorney marches to the front of the room.

"Excuse me, I was in another courtroom defending

someone else. I am Mike Moore's attorney. May we have a sidebar, Father."

My attorney just so happens to be Jesus Christ.

So the judge says yes to Jesus, who is, after all, His son. My attorney pulls His almighty Dad aside and says, "Do you remember the agreement that you and I had before the foundation of the world that whoever would receive me and believe what I did at the cross would receive eternal life? That we would wipe away all their transgressions and sins, past, present, and future?"

God nods. "Of course I remember. I am a compassionate, gracious God. I forgive all iniquities past, present, and future."

Jesus gestures toward me. "Mike is my son. He believes in me, and he's ours, Father."

The Father takes His gavel, slams it down, and says, "Case dismissed." He nods at me. "You are free to go. You are free to live your life. You are free to love others. You are now in right standing because you have been washed clean with the eternal blood of Jesus Christ. Share the truth with others. Demonstrate to them the love and mercy and generosity and compassion of the true God."

And that's it. I'm free to go. My shackles fall to my feet. My orange jumpsuit transforms into the most glorious crimson robe of righteousness. The prosecutor glares at me as I walk out of the courtroom, scot-free.

This is the power of God's love. He says "case dismissed" and that's it—it doesn't matter how many tractor-trailers there are stacked high with our sins and screw-ups. God is the master judge, the arbiter on high; but unlike the stereotype, His compassion knows no bounds.

We are His children. We are free. He has liberated us from our transgressions through His abundant love. Case dismissed.

Don't you want to step out of the courtroom of your life, shake off the sins holding you captive, and be utterly, wholly, and blissfully free?

13

BEAUTIFUL SIN CAKE

How much do you know about the Apostle Paul?

I'll tell you something that many Christians don't know: before he believed Jesus was the Messiah, Paul was helping to kill Jews who believed that Jesus was the Messiah. Yep, that's what Paul was doing. He wasn't sharing the gospel or writing loving letters chock-full of good advice. He was going around from city to city, making sure Jews were punished for confessing their belief in Yeshua (Jesus). And he was Jewish.

That's around the time Paul got whacked down by the hand of God. "Paul," the Lord said to him, "what are you doing?"

And Paul was like, "Whoa, whoa—who are you, Lord?" He was completely blindsided, and literally blinded—God shone His light so brightly that Paul could no longer see (until God restored his sight later.)

After that, Paul stopped going around giving full consent to the death of Jews who also believed Jesus was their savior, and he started believing. He began to spread the word of God, fearlessly and without restraint, an action that more than once landed him in prison.

He wrote his letter to the Philippians during one of those stints in prison. "Brothers and sisters," he says in Philippians 3:13-14, "I do not consider myself yet to have taken hold of it. But one thing I do: Forgetting what is behind and straining toward what is ahead, I press on toward the goal to win the prize for which God has called me heavenward in Christ Jesus."

Basically, Paul was saying, "I forget the past and look to the future."

When I read that, my gut response was, "How can he say that?"

It hit me like a ton of bricks. How could Paul "forget the past"? Because he had the Torah, the writings, and the prophets. And as God says through the prophet Jeremiah, "I will forgive their iniquity, and I will remember their sin no more" (Jeremiah 31:34). The very same passage that is quoted in Hebrews 8:12 and 10:17.

Whoa. It really bowled me over, reading that. God nailed every one of those sins and iniquities to the cross with His one and only Son. He forgot them completely. He's like a good friend who saw us get embarrassingly drunk last weekend and says, "Don't worry—I'll never bring it up again."

What does this mean for you and me? It means we have been freed from all regrets. There is no "should've, could've." You can stop relentlessly beating yourself up for the woman you should've married, the job you could've had, and the school you should've gone to. Maybe you're guilty of rewinding your life and obsessing over what you could have done differently. "If I hadn't gone to this party, I wouldn't have gotten arrested, and I wouldn't have this long line of regrets."

But all the while, God is up there going, "I don't know what you're talking about. I'm in control of life. If I didn't want you exactly where you are today, guess what—you wouldn't be there. I will take all the mistakes you've made—everything you've said, everything you've done, everything you shouldn't have done, everything you *think* you shouldn't have done—and mix all of that together to make the most beautiful cake you've ever seen."

Think about it. If you take a pound of flour and try to eat it, you couldn't get it down. You wouldn't eat a pound of sugar. And you'd have to be crazy to try to swallow a whole pound of butter. But if you put them all together and bake them in a pan at 350°F, you'll wolf down every bite of that delicious cake, because it's perfect.

Have you ever looked at the back of an Oriental rug? If you own one, flip it over right now and tell me what you see. It doesn't make sense, right? It looks ugly, a dull mishmash of crisscrossed threads and nonsensical patterns. But flip it back over and you've got a gorgeously intricate rug that makes your house more beautiful.

Of course the details of your life don't make sense to you, especially the ones you see as "mistakes." That's because God is weaving all this stuff together. You think you're screwing up, and meanwhile, God is going, "Relax. Your sins and your lawless deeds, I don't remember them. Stop holding yourself to the choices you think you made that were wrong. Go be free. Forget the past. There's a great big future out there. What are you doing wasting your life?"

Do you think the Apostle Paul sat around bemoaning his mistakes? Nope. He was too busy serving God and living life! He pressed on to spread the Word of the Lord, getting arrested for his actions, and writing beautiful letters to his brothers and sisters in Christ. You really think Paul could have written those letters if he hadn't been through hell first?

Paul basically said, "You know what, God? I feel like I really made a mess here. But maybe you can do something with it."

And God did. He took those ingredients and made a damn fine cake—a cake we're still taking bites of today.

As for your life and my life? They may *appear* to be a mess with tons of regrets. However, you can choose to look at your life through your glasses or through God's glasses. It makes all the difference.

Do you believe God can take all your past mistakes and weave your life into something beautiful?

Part IV

WHY DO YOU GO TO CHURCH?

14

RELIGION IS THE OPIATE OF THE PEOPLE

Religion has become a business. It's sad but true. People make money off religion, and they always have. Even back during Jesus's day, the Pharisees found endless new ways to milk people for cash or certain results, all in the name of the Lord.

It's not just that that part that gets to me. It's the way modern religion has crunched spirituality into this overly regimented, systematic box. "We're having our church service from 10:00 to 11:00 a.m. today, and we hope you show up, because that's all the time we have. From 10:00 to 10:15, we have announcements. From 10:15 to 10:45, we sing. From 10:45 to 11:00, the pastor talks. Then we pray and send you on your way." It's not just the congregation that is forced to fit into that box—it's God!

There's this attitude of, "We hope you fit into our program, God, because if you're late, we can't accommodate you." What if God shows up at 11:15 a.m.? What if at 11:15, a man who's had two knee surgeries after a torn meniscus falls to the ground and says, "I'm healed! God healed my knee!" Imagine if the pastor were to say, "Shh, the service is over, my brother. You're talking too much. Go home and come back at 10:00 a.m. next week." That's absurd!

Don't get me wrong—some churches are fantastic. But for so many of them, there's this controlling engine that sucks all the air out of the room. Even worse, it sucks all the God out of the room! And isn't God the whole reason we go to church? Are we really going to create an environment where if God is late, there's no room at the inn?

"Religion is the opiate of the people." I'm not in the habit of quoting Karl Marx, but I do think he's on to something there. For hundreds of years, people have used religion to control other people. Take Julius Caesar, whose approach was to give the people a little bread and a circus so that he could control the whole city. The people of Rome lined up at the coliseum for their fish sandwiches and their gory gladiator matches, and everybody was so gloriously distracted, nobody thought to stand up and say, "This isn't right." Throw them a party, give them entertainment, and you can do whatever you want. To some degree, this kind of control is still happening today.

If you don't think modern religion can have the same numbing effect on your conscience, think again. Today it's dressed in different clothes, and it may no longer include bloody matches to the death (at least not ones you buy tickets to), but religion whispers in our ear, "You better be careful, boy. You're going to die someday, and you'll have to pay for all your nasty sins. You better come to church, and you better be quaking in your boots the whole time, because the God of the universe is displeased with you."

No wonder religion creates a culture in which a guy is berating his wife and kids on Wednesday, but on Sunday he's right there in a church pew with the best of them. And his wife is proud of him for going to church, and he gets a nod from the pastor, and he feels pretty darn smug sitting there, pretending to listen to the word of God. And then, come Monday morning, he starts the same old cycle all over again, because nothing has really moved or changed inside him. Why? God was nowhere to be found. Would God want to set foot in that church?

Let me tell you something: Jesus loved prostitutes, tax collectors, and cheats. He knew he could reach them because they weren't pretending to be somebody they weren't. It was the Pharisees He couldn't stand, the pompous blowhards who preached their "holier-than-thou" message and constantly lorded their "religiosity" over everyone else.

As long as religion is an opiate for the masses, it's missing the main point—which is, simply, love. That's *true religion.* Love is the core of God's message, and it should fuel our worship, our sermons, and our communities. We have plenty of people in churches today who understand salvation at the cross, but then they run back under the law. "Give me a rulebook to follow," they say. And God is saying, "Stop looking for a rulebook! There's love and mercy and grace and faith. Know my love and start walking that out."

Imagine a little old lady walking across the street. When she's halfway across, she faints and falls over. Do I really need a law that says, "When women seventy and older cross the street, you're supposed to go and help them if they fall over." No! My heart moves me to go help. That's why I sprint across the street, scoop up that lady in my arms, and rush her to the nearest hospital. It's in my heart to help someone who is hurt or in danger.

Here's how I want to see the church change. I'd love it if all the pastors at all the churches around the world stood up together and said, "God, we're not sure we got it right. We see through a glass dimly.

We don't know everything. So this next year, all we're going to do is come in here and worship the Lord. We're going to come together and talk about God's goodness, His faithfulness, and His love."

You can't sell that to anyone or lord it over them. And it's a much more authentic place from which to worship the Lord God.

We all have struggles, and we all sin. How cool would it be if you went to church and your pastor said, "Everyone in this sanctuary sins. Okay, so you screwed up. God loves you. Embrace the grace of God and let's move on."

I bet if your pastor said that, you'd sit up and start paying attention! You'd stop nodding off from the opiate of religion, the ever-present message of guilt and condemnation you've been force-fed all these years. Instead, you'd show up with a renewed sense of love and faith and hope on Sunday mornings instead of numbness and dread. What a way to rip off the blinders and start living a deeply spiritual, rather than empty, religious life!

What has been your drug?

15

CHURCH IS DEAD. WHAT IF IT WEREN'T?

If I say the word "bar" to a roomful of ten people, I guarantee ten different ideas will pop into their heads. The bartender flashes immediately to a cold whiskey tonic, while the attorney sitting next to him thinks of passing the state bar exam. The former dancer thinks of doing pliés at a ballet *barre*, and the musician beside her thinks of how sheet music is measured.

The word "revival" is a lot like that. The word has many different connotations, but here's what I mean when I use it: revival occurs when God is so tired of man misrepresenting Him that He starts performing miracles and working wonders among His people. And why would He do that? Because most churches today are dead.

That's right—churches are becoming as dead as doornails. The band plays a bunch of rock songs for worship, and when it's done, the pastor gets up on stage, and he had better give a great sermon with good stories, or people are going to fall asleep. (Maybe that's why they've started putting coffee shops in churches—so the caffeine will keep people awake!) After he's done, the congregants pass around offering plates, and people walk out the door in a daze wondering, "Why didn't I *feel* anything?"

Where's the life that should be flowing through God's church? Why aren't we praying for the sick? Why aren't people getting healed inside services? That's what Jesus did and said we should expect. He didn't come to judge the world. He raised the dead, healed the sick, cast out demons, and showed kindness, grace, and mercy to the people who needed it. Talk about revival! The only ones He put aside were the Pharisees, who thought they were God's gift to man.

I think God looks at our current church services, where we've squeezed Him into a convenient 10:00 to 11:00 a.m. time slot on Sunday mornings, and thinks, "Come on! I'm getting tired of you guys misrepresenting me. I'm going to go down there and liven this church up."

So He brings in a new church member who's an

adulterer. The man falls down on his knees and cries, "I want to confess that I've been doing this my whole marriage, and God has delivered me. I can't believe how amazing this is!" Suddenly, the whole church is confessing. They're confessing to theft and slander and tax evasion and lies and gossip and webs of deceit. And the people around them are going, "That's me, too!"

Many church leaders would be disgusted by the thought of all the havoc of that scene. But that's exactly the moment God goes, "Ah, *now* I can join them. Because they're being real."

To most people today, doing the whole church thing feels like a weekly chore. So does all the stuff that goes along with being a Christian—praying, reading the Bible, and so on. Going to church is a box you check, something you have to do. People see God as this all-knowing accountant, someone who's keeping track of when you punch in and out.

Besides, what will the other parishioners say if you're not at church? Will they gossip about you behind your back?

What happened to going to church as an act of love or service? What would it be like if the pastor stood up in front and said, "Hey everybody, listen up for a sec. Follow your heart. If you don't want to come to church, fine. Stay home, drink coffee, be with your family." How would people respond if their pastor said that? Would they stop living in fear of being judged? If a pastor said that, how many people would enjoy showing up?

How would people act if they weren't living in fear of being judged?

Recently I got called in for jury duty.

"Mr. Moore," the attorney said to me. "Do you think you can render a correct judgment?"

"Judge what?" I asked.

"Can you judge this man right here?"

"No," I said, shaking my head. "I can't judge any man. If you were asking me to judge his behavior, that's one thing. But if you want me to judge him, you're talking to the wrong guy."

That pissed the lawyer off, as you might imagine. He asked me some more questions, and eventually I said, "You know what? This man is the only one who knows, in his heart, whether he committed this crime or not. And it's really sad that we have to get twelve of his peers to sit down and have attorneys cross-examine him to try to get to the truth, since he won't say it."

At that point the attorney wheeled around and said to the judge, "Your honor, I'd like to exercise your vote to not have this man be on the jury."

Fair enough. But I stand by my conviction. That guy on trial for murder is the only guy who knows if he did it. Only he and God.

God looks into our hearts. He's the only one who can see the why behind the what. So why try to trick Him into thinking we want to go to church if we don't? He knows we don't want to be there. He's patiently standing by, reminding us, "I'm okay with it. Go home."

What would you rather be doing than going to a dead church? Do what makes you happy, not what you have to do. If you can't get to the point in your life when you get to pray for the sick, then don't. Whatever you do only out of obligation, stop doing it right now.

I wonder how radically different our churches would be if we actually wanted to be there. Whatever you're doing because of fear of man, because people are watching you, because your conscience says you have to, because you think God will punish you or be mad at you if you don't—what if you could get rid of all that?

What would you do then? How would your Sundays be different?

16

THE THING ABOUT CHURCH AND HOOKERS

So there's this guy who wants his wife to know how much he loves her.

"I love you so much, baby," he says. "You're an amazing woman. I mean, I've never met anybody like you. I'm so blessed to be with someone like you. You're just wonderful."

The wife likes the way this is going so far, so she is understandably shocked by the next words that come out of her husband's mouth.

"Listen," he says. "I need two hours to go out and be with a hooker, okay? But I'll be right back because I want to spend all the time I can with you, baby. That's how much I love you."

What do you think the wife's reaction would be? Depends on the wife, of course, but he could get anything from a slap across the face to a call from the divorce lawyer!

The man is saying, "I love you, I love you, I love you," but there's no action behind those words. What are words without true action behind them? They're lies, empty and meaningless.

And that, sadly enough, is the same reason most people go to church. They're paying lip service to what they love, just like the guy pays lip service to his wife when he'd really rather be out with a hooker. Our "hookers" may look different than his, but if going to church is really just reciting empty words with no actions behind them, we're no better than that poor schmuck.

For the most part, people don't go to church because they want to go; they go so they can check a box. They go because their conscience is nagging them. "Shoot," they say to themselves, "I'm supposed to believe in what I say I believe in. And if I believe, there's got to be some kind of behavior behind it. I can't just *say* I believe in God and then avoid His house every Sunday like the plague."

So week after week, people drag themselves to church, especially on the big holidays like Christmas and Easter. I once knew a little girl who astutely pointed out that there were dozens of people who would show up at church on those two days, people she never saw the rest of the year. "Chreasters," she called them, which sounded spot-on to me.

I like to ask people, "What are you passionate about? What is the thing that drives you in life?" Believe me, most people I ask don't say, "Oh, I'm passionate about going to church, Mike! It's a driving force in my life."

I'll shoot straight with you: if you as a human being aren't touched at the core by being there on Sunday mornings, then why the hell do you make yourself do it?

I love what Solomon said. "Out of the abundance of the heart, the mouth speaks." Next time you're around your buddies or your coworkers, listen to what they talk about, because that's what they really believe. If Steve is always talking about being out on the boat, the guy's passionate about boating. He'd probably rather be out on a boat on Sunday morning than in a pew at church.

You know what God has to say about that? "Go on your boat, Steve. Be happy. What do you need to come to church for? I'm on the boat. I'm also on the water. I'm all over the place. Serve me in your boat, the place you love, not in church, the place you hate." So many people go to church because of guilt and obligation, and those aren't the reasons God wants you there. Far from it.

Now, I'm speaking generally, of course. There are

certainly men and women who love going to church, who say, "You know what? I want to be around a group of people who believe the same things I do. I want to sing and listen to a great sermon that helps me make it through the week." There are people like that too, and good for them.

But is church the one and only meeting ground for us to grow in our relationship with God? NO. Capital N, capital O. Church should be the "overflow" from our personal time with Christ, meaning the time we spend reading the Scriptures or engaging with family and friends. It should be more of a fellowship, the happy hour we get to spend every week around like-minded people.

But if Sunday is the only time and place I get fed? The one place where I get my meat for the week? That's not enough. It's like if I said, "Come over to my house on Sunday, and I'll feed you a nice steak and a bottle of wine, but you don't get to eat again until next Sunday." That's not sustainable—you gotta eat every day.

It's no different with the Spirit. You gotta eat every day. This isn't 400 BC or 50 AD, when you had to go to the synagogue to hear the Scripture. Back then, there weren't little Torahs printed out on pieces of paper you could take home and read at night. So if you wanted to hear God's word, you went to the synagogue. Otherwise, you wouldn't know what He said.

These days, we all can have the Word of God sitting on our coffee tables! And yet we go to church on Sundays because we gotta hear what the guy has to say? If you have your own Bible, read it yourself!

Do you come to church to pray? Pray at home! Pray everywhere.

Say you're driving down the street. Try this prayer on for size: "Lord, thank you that I can drive an automobile. Thank you for being with me no matter where I go." Boom. There's a prayer.

"Lord, I pray for my buddy in the hospital. Just raise him up, Lord. Heal him. I don't want him to die. He's too young. He's got a family." Boom. There's another one.

If you need church to pray, you're in a big world of hurt. If you need church to listen to what God says, to hear His Word, you're hurting, my friend. Go to church to be around likeminded people, to worship God in a community of people. Don't go to church when you'd really rather be somewhere—anywhere—else. That's like staring at your wife, swearing you love her, when you're really thinking about the hooker down the street!

If you felt like you had complete freedom, what would you do?

17

CHURCH: THE WORST MANAGER YOU'LL EVER HAVE

When did we, as human beings, decide that some things we do are worse than others in God's mind?

If you cheat on your wife, practice same-sex marriage, watch pornography incessantly—whatever that list is—we go, "Wow. That's awful." The church is adamant about the issues it chooses: homosexuality, pornography, divorce, adultery, and so on. If you drink too much, there's an AA group for you. There are groups for sex and porn addiction.

But we never address gossip, anger, unforgiveness, pride, arrogance, conceit... There's not a GA for Gossipers Anonymous. There's not a PA for Pride Anonymous. How about UA, for Unforgiveness Anonymous? Why aren't we forming groups for those sins?

All we're trying to do with these support groups is

manage external behavior. The real reason we don't have GA or PA or UA is because it's hard to manage those sorts of things. But we can manage whether or not you're looking at porn or sleeping with your neighbor's wife.

The more we try to manage external behavior, the more we miss out on the heart of the Father. Changed behavior without a changed heart behind it is like doing open-heart surgery without the heart. If you don't change the thing at the center of the problem—the organ pumping blood to all the other organs and keeping the body alive—then what's the point?

That's why the modern church has it all wrong. Trying to get people to behave a certain way without a change of heart is a surefire recipe for creating a group of bitter, angry, religious people who nobody wants to be around. God is up there saying, "Why won't anybody walk around sharing the fact that I'm good and compassionate and merciful and kind? Why aren't my children down there shouting about how I forgive iniquity, transgression, and sin?"

A few months ago, I spoke to nine hundred high school students. The kids went home and talked about some of the stuff I said to their parents, a couple of whom called the school principal.

"We want to meet with this Mike Moore guy," they said. "He said some things that we've never heard before. Some unbelievable things."

So I went and sat down with the forty or so parents who showed up. They asked me to share some of the stuff with them that I'd shared with their kids, but instead I told them, "I have nothing to talk to you about. I only have questions for you." And so I started to ask questions.

"Why would God take a twenty-year-old with all that testosterone and stick him in a church where the pastor and everybody says, 'Okay, you can't look at porn, you can't look at any nude women, you can't touch yourself, don't go near it, don't think about it,' thereby making sure that those things will definitely happen? After hearing that, kids will get together when they're by themselves, talk about sex, and do their own thing and experiment. Then they'll get caught, and they'll be in trouble. Why would God set His children up for that?"

Nobody spoke. No one had an answer to my question.

Why do we, as a church body, treat people like they're sick or off-base? Why don't we treat human beings as human?"

It's time we started asking the right questions, even if they're the ones we're all afraid to ask. Even if we don't have the answers.

What do you want to ask God? Right now, if He

were in front of you, what would be your question? How would He answer you?

Part V

INTRODUCING THE DEFENDER

18

DO WE REALLY NEED A GO-BETWEEN?

Most of the world's religions are built on the idea that you need an intercessor between you and God. The church says you need a priest or minister or pastor praying for you, or more accurately, praying *at* you. It's been this way for thousands of years. Religion has always tried to make us believe we need a "go-between."

I want you to picture, for a moment, two warring nations that go into battle. Nation A and Nation B are fighting one another, as they've done for hundreds of years—but the truth is, they don't really want to. So as the approaching armies climb atop their respective mountains, each nation sends an ambassador down into the valley below. Both ambassadors amble down the side of the mountain and meet in the valley to negotiate the terms of peace.

What is Nation A's guarantee that Nation B will do what it said? The ambassador. The same goes for Nation B—the people of Nation B have put their faith in Nation A's man. Both nations are dependent on their ambassadors to negotiate for peace. So the men write down their terms and sign the papers. Nation A feels like it has a guarantee that Nation B will do what it said it would do, and vice versa. They have to trust that the ambassadors are telling the truth.

But what if Nation A is lying to Nation B? Or what if Nation B is pulling the wool over Nation A's eyes and preparing a massive ambush? It's certainly possible. Welcome to international relations—everyone has hidden agendas and vested interests. It's a real shame that the word "diplomacy" has come to mean how good you are at lying to the other team.

But what if those ambassadors were the same? What if Nation A's ambassador fully represented Nation A, *while also fully representing* Nation B? It would be perfect, actually. It would be a perfect scenario in which everyone was fairly served.

What is God's guarantee to mankind? Jesus Christ. God sent His son to represent Himself on planet Earth. Jesus walked the earth for thirty-three years, was crucified, died, and was resurrected as fully God and fully man. So we have God representing Himself to man and man representing himself to God, and they're both the same. It's perfect.

To go back to our example, if both nations had the same ambassador, and that ambassador could represent both sides perfectly, peace would undoubtedly be restored. And when it comes to the battle of the human spirit, this is exactly the gift that's been granted us. It's why we don't need another go-between—the only "intercessor" we need is God Himself. The first time God came to that valley as the ambassador of love and life, He came as a suffering servant. The second time, He will come as a conquering king. And so the representatives of man to God and God to man are the same person. Perfect justice, perfect love.

There is one mediator between God and man: the Lord Jesus Christ. That means you don't need anyone else! The best thing about Jesus being the intercessor for us is that He's never unreachable. We don't have to "take a number" or see His personal assistant about scheduling. He's just right there, whenever we need Him, even at 3:00 a.m. We don't need anyone to mediate for us. In truth, there's no one who can. God has already done all the mediating for you so that you can live free. The battle for your soul has already been won—all you have to do is claim your identity in Christ.

So take off your armor and come down off that mountain. The battle for your soul has already been won.

The problem is that we really don't believe that these terms of peace are permanent. We think that somehow we can "screw this up." But what if we couldn't? What if it were a solid covenant that won't change? How would that affect the way we view ourselves? Better yet, would we finally see how He views us?

19

OUR IDENTITY IS IN CHRIST

We all want to identify with something. What is our identity? Who are we? In this crazy world, every one of us is looking for an identity that suits us. We all want to *be* somebody.

How many ways are there for human beings to identify on this planet? We say, "Well, this is who I am. I do this. My résumé looks like this. I have this much money. I work out in the gym, and that's my identity." Or, "I know this person." Or, "This is my title at work." There's nothing wrong with those things. But our *true* identity is in Christ. That's why we are here—to reconnect to God in Christ Jesus.

When a person puts their faith and trust in Christ, it's as simple as, "Dear Jesus, forgive me for my sin. I don't have complete understanding of all this, but I believe what you did for me at the cross, and I believe that you satisfied the Father by what you did for me. I am putting my trust and my faith in you. Come into my heart." When we do this, we are reconnected to the Father. Our identity is in Christ, and we receive the gift of the Holy Spirit.

I read a story once in which the Americans set up a lot of orphanages in France after World War II. One bitter cold evening, a man came to an orphanage with his daughter. Their shoes were worn, and their faces were dirty—obviously neither one had eaten in a very long time. They were disheveled, their clothes old and torn, their ribs sticking out through thin shirts. The little girl in particular looked very pale and weak.

The woman in charge of the orphanage came to the door. "May I help you?" she asked the man with his frail daughter.

"I understand that you take in children," said the man.

"That is correct, sir. That is what we are trying to do, to the best of our ability."

"Would you take my daughter, please? You can see she's … look at her. She's about to die. And I wanted to bring her here because I know you will help her."

"Well, sir," the woman said carefully. "As you can see, this is an orphanage, and we have so many people coming in. This is really a haven for children who have no mother or father, and we have to draw the line somewhere. You are her father, and there are just so many other children who do not have parents at all."

"But look at my daughter," the man begged. "How can you do this? Just look at her. She needs help."

"Sir, we understand, and we are so sorry. There's just nothing we can do."

"So what you're telling me," the man said, "is that you would accept my daughter into your orphanage, and she would be able to eat every day, she'd have a warm bed, she'd have clothes … if I wasn't around? If I died?"

The woman hesitated and then nodded. "I'm afraid those are the rules."

"Okay," said the man. "I understand." He took his daughter gently in his arms and said, "Honey, look at me. I want you to know I love you."

Then he turned and stepped into the street, right into the path of an American tanker. He killed himself so that his daughter could have life.

That reminds me in a profound way of what Jesus Christ did. He gave himself up so we could get our lives back.

So many people just exist in the world today. You can exist in life just because you're alive and your body keeps moving around and you're doing activities. You can exist as a billionaire, driving a Rolls Royce. You can exist as a jetsetter, flying all over the world and enjoying yourself. You can exist on the street as a bum. You can exist as many, many kinds of people—but you cannot truly *live* until you are reconnected to your source. And you are reconnected to your source only when you put your trust and faith in the Lord Jesus Christ.

You may feel like you've heard this before.

If you fly a lot, whether for business or pleasure, you hear a lot of the same messages over and over. "Ladies and gentlemen, welcome to Flight 467, non-stop from Dallas to New York's LaGuardia Airport. Once we reach our cruising altitude of 34,000 feet, the captain will turn off the fasten seatbelt sign, indicating you are free to move about the cabin. But once you are seated, keep your seatbelt securely fastened as we may encounter unexpected turbulence. An information card has been provided in the seatback in front of you."

How many times have we all heard these words, this same message on repeat? Maybe five hundred times, over the course of our lifetimes. But how often do we actually *listen* to it?

"If there is a sudden change in cabin pressure, the mask compartment located above your seat will open automatically. When this happens, quickly reach for the nearest mask." That's funny. "Quickly." Like I'm going to stall if I'm dying for air.

"Please ensure the plastic bag is clear of the mask, and place the yellow cup over your nose and your mouth. Continue to breathe normally." Now, if we're in a tailspin, I doubt I'm going to continue to breathe normally!

I once asked a flight attendant, "When you're sharing these safety precautions, how many people in the cabin make eye contact with you?"

"Sir, I've been doing this for fifteen years, and maybe one person looks at me," she said. "Most people are business travelers, and they hear it over and over and over and over and over. They don't pay a bit of attention. But let me tell you a story.

"One time the yellow masks came down. Something happened and the pressure was cut in half. And this gentleman in first class leapt out of his seat, ran up to me, and said, 'My God, we're gonna die.' He was freaking out. This man had been on a plane a billion times. He'd heard this message over and over and over again. We said, 'Sir, would you please sit down?' 'I can't sit down. What am I supposed to do? These yellow things fell out. What do I do?' 'Sir, please sit down!'

"I took him back to his seat and put the oxygen mask around his head, and he started breathing normally. Everything was fine, even though he had totally freaked out. We were never in any danger. But how many times had he heard that message and yet never paid attention? What if something *had* gone wrong? He wouldn't have had the faintest idea what to do!"

It's the same thing with us. How many times have we heard from people, "Are you a Christian? You must be born again." Maybe the message of God's love came to us in a negative way, but maybe not. Maybe we just heard it one too many times. But we have to listen, because it's the most important message we will ever hear. It's the only message that will grant us eternal life.

The gift of eternal life is 100 percent free. He wants to give that to us. And all we have to do is put our trust and our faith in Him. When we reconnect to the Father, we reclaim our identity in Christ. And believe me when I say a connected existence is better than anything we can experience on this planet without Him.

So reclaim your identity. Give over to God. And then, like that little girl at the orphanage, be fed. Find a church that teaches the Bible as the Word of God, a real (not boring) church, where you know you're going to get fed. If you're eating hamburger now, go find a church that's teaching a nice New York bone-in strip steak. Take that new bone and gnaw the hell out of it. Let God do some things in your life. He will guide you and direct you. Just ask Him.

Do you want Him to show you who you truly are?

20

FLIP ON THE SWITCH

I was recently at a wealthy gentleman's home in Houston. It's a beautiful home, situated on six acres, overlooking a stunning lake. I was there for a barbecue, and this gentleman was kind enough to give us a tour of his gorgeous home.

When we got to the master suite, he took us into the closet. Now, this was not a normal closet. This closet was huge. I couldn't believe it. A family of four could live in his closet. But in the corner was this huge metal door with one of those big wheels on it, the kind they use on a bank vault. This wheel was particularly cool because it said Fort Knox on it.

"Wow," I said. "This sure is a cool room."

"It gets even better," he said, and opened up the heavy door to reveal another room, about ten feet by ten feet. This guy was a cement contractor, so the walls were eight inches thick with steel plates in between. This place couldn't have been safer.

"If a tornado were to come, this would be the safest place for us to be. We'd go in here."

A thought struck me. If a tornado were to come, and let's say it did indeed hit this man's home, as long as his family was inside that vault, they would be safe. They trusted the vault to save them. As long as they were in the vault, they were safe from the tornado because the vault had been made to protect them.

Isn't that exactly what God did for us in Christ?

To put our trust in Christ means stepping out of ourselves and not trusting our own good works to save us or our own abilities to secure eternal life. Instead, we transfer that trust to Jesus Christ's act of dying on the cross. We say, "Jesus, I believe that you satisfied the Father completely. That's why you died for me. You took away all my sins when you died on the cross."

When Jesus died, all our sins were in his future. Our past sins, our present sins, even the sins we'll commit ten years from now—all of it was in his future. And when he conquered death through his resurrection, it was the guarantee that all was all taken care of. He's alive today! And when we put our trust in Him, we're basically saying, "I have to get out of myself and put my trust in what Jesus Christ did for me." That's what it means to put your trust in someone else.

My money is in a bank. When I go to make a demand against what I have in my account, I'm trusting that my money is safe in that bank. That's putting my trust in something outside of myself.

The utility that brings electricity to my home is Texas Utilities. Can this company provide electricity? Yes, because that's what it does. Will the company do so? Yes, it will. In fact it's already done so. The electricity to my home is already provided for, because I pay for it.

At least, that's what I thought until one night a few weeks ago.

I got home late after a long week of travel. It was 11:00 p.m., dark as pitch, and I was stumbling around, bumping into things. And I was thinking, "I can't believe Texas Utilities. This is unbelievable. What a bunch of fakes. What a bunch of phonies."

So I finally got to the phone and dialed the number to Texas Utilities. I was spitting mad. Some kid in the call center picked up.

"Is this Texas Utilities?" I said.

"Yes, it is, sir."

"You know what? You guys are a bunch of fakes."

"Sir, what do you mean?"

"I come to my home and I pay my bills on time,

and you guys say that I'm supposed to have electrical service to my home and it's pitch black in here."

"Sir, we have done everything we can to provide electricity to your home. We can't do any more than we have already done for you. Sir, can I ask you a question?" Deep breath. "Have you flipped on the switch yet?"

"Um, wait. You mean, I had to *do* something?"

"Yes, sir. All you have to do is flip the switch on, and the electricity will be there for you."

And then I realized—I hadn't turned on the lights. I'd been so busy stumbling around in the dark and cursing my electric company that I forgot to flip the freakin' switch!

"Oh, gee. Sorry, guys. Sounded kinda stupid and crazy there, didn't I?"

But you know what? That's exactly what God did for us. He has provided everything for us already, yet so many of us stumble around in the dark, cursing His name. God cannot do any more than He's already done in Christ. He has provided it fully. Our job is to believe and flip the switch on. Texas Utilities says my electricity is there. How do I know that? How do I believe what the company says? How do I know there's electricity in my home? I walk over to my wall and I flip on the switch.

How do I know God has provided for me already? How do I know Jesus is who he said he was and that he is going to forgive me? That he is going to give me peace and joy? That he's going to love me unconditionally like I've never been loved before? How do I know Jesus Christ is going to reconnect me to God?

Because God said so. All I have to do is walk over, ask Jesus Christ to forgive me for my sins, and flip on the switch.

"But Mike, how do I know it's true?" you say.

Well, how do I know Texas Utilities is true? Because it said so. And because I walk over to that light switch and flip it on.

We are talking about the God of the universe. He cannot lie. He says to us, "Remember the greatest need is the forgiveness of sin, and I want to forgive you for all your sins. I want you to be reconnected to me. That's why I sent my son." And all you have to do is say, "Lord, I believe that." And flip on the switch.

Now that is powerful—more powerful than any ol' tornado or electric current!

That kind of faith is not stupid, unintelligent, or unwise; nor is it an uneducated guess. Rather, it is the opposite on all counts!

Do you believe that the greatest need of the human heart is the forgiveness of sin?

Part VI

GRACE
(FINALLY FREE)

21

GOD'S DOGS

My little niece and nephew have a dog named Molly.
She follows them around wherever they go. The other
day I used Molly to teach them about God's love.

"Molly follows you guys everywhere because she
loves you," I told them. "She's going to run after you
wherever you go."

I told them about an article I'd read recently in the
paper. A dog was stolen from Dallas and brought to
Oklahoma City. That's about two and a half hours by
car—a hundred and fifty miles, give or take. It took
the dog a long time, but he walked all the way back to
Dallas and made his way home.

"Dogs can always find their owners," I said to my
niece and nephew. "The dogs are going, 'Where's my
love? Where's my food?' And they won't stop until

they've found you."

Goodness and mercy are God's dogs. God says, "I don't care what you've done. You can't get away from my mercy and goodness. You just can't!"

It doesn't matter what you do or where you go—God's goodness and mercy will track you down all the days of your life, just like a loving dog.

If that is true because God says it, then wouldn't we want to take the time to get to know these animals?

What breed is goodness? What color is mercy? What are these qualities like? What do they look like?

They will not rest until they are in your lap and you are petting them. Don't you want to get to know these dogs?

22

RIGHTEOUS, DUDE

Do you think of yourself as righteous?

Let me ask you another question: Do you think of yourself as self-righteous?

You'd probably say "yes" to the first question long before you'd say "yes" to the second. But if you're like most people, you constantly confuse the two.

Maybe you are someone who has a list of things that you know God wants you to follow, and you've done a pretty good job keeping them so far. Your list might go something like "I've never cheated on my wife. I've never looked at porn. I don't cheat on my taxes. I constantly tell the truth. And if I say I'm going to be somewhere at 6:00 p.m. and I get there at 6:15, I automatically call myself a liar." I know people like this—in fact I used to be one of them. I was the kind of guy who held himself to rigid standards. If I could check everything off that list, I felt like I was doing great. I felt righteous.

But that isn't righteousness—that's *self*-righteousness. The way God uses the word "righteous" in the scriptures is actually this: Righteousness isn't doing the right thing. It's *being* the right thing.

A man doesn't arrive at righteousness as if it were a destination. God *makes* him righteous. Genesis 15:6 says, "Then [Abraham] believed in the Lord and He counted it to him as righteousness."

I once had a great conversation with a guy in Starbucks about this.

"How could God make Abraham righteous prior to the giving of the law?" I asked him.

"Because he believed," the guy said. "That's righteousness by faith. Abraham believed what God said, and God said, 'I'll make you righteous.' It's a gift."

Righteousness is not something for us to do or decide or attain. It is a gift we are given when we believe in the Lord Jesus. God was basically saying to Abraham, "I will do for you what you can't do for yourself."

Remember the example of the drowning man? If you're in the water drowning and you can't swim, you can't save yourself. There is nothing you can do unless somebody pulls you out of the water. And that's what Jesus came to do. He didn't come to judge you—he came to pull you out, dry you off, and save your life. All you have to do is receive the gospel. And that's when you truly become righteous.

When I was a *self*-righteous dude, sticking stubbornly to that list of rules, I had the most sterile relationship with the Lord on the planet. My list was standing between my heavenly Father's love and me. I was always holding up that list going, "Because of this, you love me, God!"

And God was going, "In spite of that, I love you."

Back when I hadn't yet learned this lesson, I inflicted my self-righteousness on others. I wouldn't let guys come to my Bible study if they were divorced. I was twenty-eight years old, and I thought I knew everything. When one of my Bible study members told me he and his wife were moving painfully toward divorce, I said to him, "If you leave your wife, you cannot come to my Bible study, because you should be questioning your Christianity." That's how tough I was about doing the right thing.

And then three years later, at thirty-one, I was a Bible study leader who found himself getting a divorce. The unthinkable had happened: *I* was leaving my wife. Back then, you had to stand before a judge to get a divorce, so I did, and he said, "Michael, I will grant your divorce." I swear, I walked out of that courthouse and heard a tiny little voice asking me, "So, Mike, tell me—are you a Christian?"

This voice whacked me upside the head like a two-by-four. I knew it was God speaking to me. And He said, "Guess what? You still are. And so is that guy you kicked out of your Bible study."

And then God said, "I want you to experience my love."

But I couldn't accept it. I didn't think I deserved it. "This isn't who I think I am in Christianity," I said. "And it's not your view of me, God. It says in Malachi you hate divorce." I had done the exact opposite of what God said!

"I also hate gossip," He said, "and you do that a lot, too. There are plenty of things you do that I don't like. You don't even realize it. But I love you. I sent my son to die for you out of pure love. No conditions, no strings attached. I chose you, and I have made you righteous."

It really blew me away, hearing that. Those rules I carried around made me feel like a good person, but actually I was still a sinful person, even when I had checked off every one. I was the same person then that I was when I walked out of that courthouse a newly divorced man. And *God still loved me.*

Believing that fact will change what you do.

If you carry your own list around, you're probably doing the same thing. "Look here, God!" you say, waving it in front of Him like a kid proud of her report card. "Look at all the good stuff I've done! I'm doing all the right things!"

But you can't do all the right things. It's impossible. You've got a sinful nature, just like all the rest of us. Do you realize that outside of Jesus Christ, outside of your belief in God, you have the same nature as Adolf Hitler? It sounds horrible, but you have the same capacity for evil as he did, because you are both flawed human beings.

Now, you may not carry out this capacity for evil— and let's hope you never do. But like it or not, that is your nature. And that's what Jesus died for. Your old self has been buried with Christ, and you have been resurrected into a new woman or man. God put His nature in you.

That's why I tell people they have to break the lists they carry around, the lists that make them feel (self-) righteous. Your list has to die. And what I've found is that people can't kill their list until they realize they've already violated it. If you never lie, you need to experience lying or exaggerating. If you're never late, you need to be egregiously, unforgivably late. Then you can start to see the unconditioned, unmerited, and utterly underserved love and grace of God.

I'm not saying go out and do things for the sake of doing them. Are we to continue sinning so that Grace will get bigger? No!

When your list becomes the intermediary between you and God, you've negated the cross and what it actually means. So if violating your list is the only way for you to get back into a direct relationship with God, then violate it!

Are you ready to trash your list?

23

LIGHTEN THE LOAD

I met a Christian woman the other day, a committed wife and mother. She was really suffering.

"My son is in the hospital," she told me. "He has a brain tumor. He's eight." This woman looked at me with tears in her eyes. "What did I do wrong for God to punish me like this? He must be trying to show me something about myself."

I looked at her and felt such compassion. This poor woman was suffering enough as it was, and in addition to the pain of what her family was going through, she was convinced God was punishing her!

"The God you're talking about?" I said. "I know nothing about him. A God who inflicts a tumor on your son to punish you? That's not the God of the universe. My God would never put a tumor in your son's head because of something you did wrong. If that's the case, then you and I do not serve the same God."

"Then why would God—your God—do this?" she asked.

I'm not going to lie; there's not an easy answer to that question. We all want to know why bad things happen, and I can talk about it for days on end and still feel sad and confused.

Here's what I do understand: because of sin, we are all living in a world of good and evil. We inherited this world from our forefathers, all the way back to Adam and Eve. Although each of us gets to make choices in life, even if we make the best possible set of choices, we cannot avoid the evil and the pain and the suffering that run rampant on this earth.

What we *can* do is choose to understand that these are not punishments or proof of God's wrath. God was not punishing this poor woman. Far from it—He wanted to wrap her up in His arms of gentle, tender love.

In the midst of so much grief and sadness, I did what little I could to lighten the load: I spoke with her for hours about God's tremendous grace and undying love.

But is that enough? All this woman wanted was for her son to be well, and I couldn't make that happen. I could pray and believe for his healing, but what else could I do? Blame God? Or is there something else?

24

GIVE IT AWAY

If I have $50 million in cash, and there's a guy who needs four dollars, I'm going to give the guy four bucks. If I own a dealership and have fifty million automobiles, and I find out one of my employees is walking thirty miles a day just to get to work, I'm going to give the guy a car. Because of what's been given to me, I have to give it away. I don't have a choice, if I truly understand why I own what I have.

The other day I was getting off the elevator at work, and a lady asked me, "Can I ask you a question? Why are you always so happy?"

"You can't handle the answer," I said, and kept walking.

A few days later, I saw her on the elevator again. "You are an amazing woman," I said. "You just are."

She looked surprised. "You don't even know me."

"I don't need to know you. You're the most unique person on the planet. You have fingerprints that no one else has. Everything you touch, God's touching through you. How cool is that?"

I started to get off the elevator, but she pushed the button to keep it open. "Hold on," she said. "You're not leaving. Tell me what is going on."

"If you knew that all your sins were forgiven—past, present, and future—how could you not be happy?"

"Whoa," she said. "I didn't expect that."

"I know you didn't," I said. "That's why I said you couldn't handle it!"

But that's the reality. Why am I so happy? Because I'm walking around with a clean slate! Past, present, and future, I'm sinless in God's eyes because of what Christ did for me. I'm going to heaven when I die. And I want to give everyone I meet the same opportunity.

Let's say I'm a surgeon and I meet a man with a malignant tumor. We meet in a business context, but we become friends. I go to his home for dinner and meet his wife. He tells me about his tumor. "That's awful," I say. "I'm so sorry." And then I go about my life, and the guy dies.

I'm a doctor. I could have removed that tumor for him. All I needed to say was, "By the way, I'm a surgeon. I remove tumors for a living. Come to my office and we'll sit down and talk. No charge."

Who knows? The man might not be interested in what I have to say. He could say, "No thanks. I'm going to die from this tumor. That's just the way it is." But I at least have to try.

I'm a master in the art of living, and it has nothing to do with me. It's not about me. It's about what Christ did, and it's about my faith in what He did. How can I not be happy? And how can I not share that with other people? It's too good. I can't hoard that for myself. I've got to give it away.

The fact is, whatever we truly believe we give away every day of our lives...we are wearing it on our sleeve. Listen to what you say to people, and then ask yourself why you are saying it the way you are. You are either giving all day long what you believe or giving the opposite of what you believe to protect it—but you are giving it!

By the way, what is a master in the art of living anyway? Around 1930, a man named L.P. Jacks, full of life experience at the age of seventy, said it this way:

A master in the art of living makes no distinction between his work and his play; his labor and his leisure; his mind and his body; his education and his recreation. He hardly knows which is which. He simply pursues his vision of excellence in whatever he is doing and leaves it to others to determine whether he is working or playing. Because to him it feels like he is doing both!

Are you ready to become a master in the art of living? Start practicing the giving of grace.

25

GO ON, GET OFFENDED

The other day I was speaking at a men's group about grace. We were coming to a close when one of the guys raised his hand.

"You know, Mike," he began, "I'm not sure I agree with any of this. I don't think you're doing it right. As a matter of fact, I think you're lying about a lot of it. You make it all seem so warm and fuzzy, like we can do anything we want—lie, cheat, steal, even kill—and God will give us milk and a cookie."

If you think I got mad or surly, think again. I just grinned at the guy.

"You know," I said, "that's the biggest compliment I've gotten in my two years here. If I'm teaching properly, I'm going to offend somebody. So I'm glad to hear I offended you! But it isn't actually *me* that offended you. It's God's truth. And if what I've said offends you, it's probably because your belief system needs some offending."

As you can imagine, that ruffled his feathers quite a bit.

There were forty men in this group, and I turned to address them all. "I want everybody here to listen," I said. "Let's go at it. Let's really get into this, because this is what it's all about."

That's the kind of guy I am. To understand truth, I think you sometimes have to go to extremes to get it. That's the only way you're going to know where you truly stand.

So we really got into it, this guy and I. Everything I said to him about God's grace he would turn back around on me. "Yeah, but what about this?" he'd say, brandishing his Bible. "What about when God says, 'Don't do this'? Or when He tells the people of Israel, 'You can't do that'?"

"Let's back up," I said. "Remember that God spoke to the children of Israel through the prophet Jeremiah. He told them He was going to make a new covenant with the House of Israel. God said, 'I will write my law in their hearts. Their sins and their lawless deeds, I will remember no more.'"

It's in Psalms 103, too. God says, "I have not dealt with you according to your sin, and I have not punished you according to your iniquities." God is basically saying, "I'm not like you. I don't hold grudges. You are making me out to be someone I'm not." God is saying He will forget our iniquities and wash away our sins. The slate has been wiped clean.

I explained this to the guys in the group. God is not sitting up in heaven like an angry six-year-old, saying, "Eh, you did it again. You better say you're sorry because you just keep screwing up." The cross was a one-time event. Jesus died for our sins so that the slate would be wiped clean forever.

Our sins were either handled on the cross or they weren't. Jesus's last three words were, "It is finished." The atonement for sin was finished. One time. Once and for all. *Done.* Never to be brought up again.

But according to this guy in the group, it wasn't finished. He kept saying, "But what about when you fall back into sin?"

"You fall out of a boat into the water," I told him. "You don't fall back into sin. You're either in or you're out.

"Now, if you want to keep count of your sins against yourself," I said, "I can't help you with that. You're blind to the truth. The truth will make you free—you just can't see it yet."

At which point the guy got mad enough that he started calling me names. He was really angry. One of the guys tried to put a stop to it, but I told him to let the guy be. I don't mind anger. Sometimes it's the fastest way to the truth.

At the end of the conversation, this guy was in exactly the same place as he was when we started. And it was time to go. I couldn't keep the rest of the guys there forever. So we ended in prayer, as usual, and I let the group know that if they wanted to talk more about this, I'd be available afterwards.

After we were done and people started to leave, I walked over to the guy who'd started the discussion and gave him a big hug. I could tell he felt bad that he'd let his temper get the best of him.

"Hey man, it's cool," I said. "This is probably going to be the most pompous, arrogant thing you've ever heard, but I used to be where you are at right now. I sat there thinking, 'This is too good to be true. It's not real. God is not that good.' So I know where you're coming from. Here's the thing: You can come at me as much as you want. You can keep telling me God isn't who I say He is. You're not bothering me, because God is strong enough that He doesn't need Mike Moore to defend Him."

Listen, I know this can be misunderstood. But God's a lion. He can defend Himself. I don't have to defend Him. And if His truth offends you? Good. Go on, get offended. All it means is that God's truth is starting to work its way into your heart.

When we operate in our own wisdom and see with our own eyes, then our perception (keyword) of good and evil is in the context of shame, fear, and hiding. We interpret so as to cover ourselves or condemn ourselves before He condemns us.

In this refuge of self-condemnation, reaching for mercy and grace feels like the ultimate act of rebellion because the self-condemnation feels so right and just.

God responds, "Why do my people who seek me forsake me to find me?"

We forsake the cross of Jesus Christ to find Him elsewhere. We beg Him to punish us so that we might feel forgiven, but He already punished His son for us. Essentially we seek Him in the "light" of our own self-contempt, turning Him into an image of our own fallen selves because His true image is so foreign to us. When eating from the fruit of the tree of knowledge, we reject the Grace that escapes our reason. We refuse to accept what we don't deserve because we don't understand. In doing so, we cling to what we do understand with our own eyes: judgment for our sins. We walk in a wrath for which we are not destined.

Are you ready to be freed from this false system of belief?

What would you do for this kind for freedom?

There is nothing to do!

Part VII

YOU DON'T LIKE ME BECAUSE YOU DON'T KNOW ME

♥ | ⛪

26

BABY, TAKE OUT THE TRASH

How much does it hurt us when we fail to recognize another person's point of view?

The answer varies depending on the situation, but it can hurt a lot. It's the reason friendships fail and marriages flounder. We're all used to living in our own heads and hearts, believing that we know "the way it is," the definitive truth. We forget that other people have their own perspectives—and "the way it is" for them is often very different than "the way it is" for us.

I had an opportunity a few years ago to be the best man at a friend's wedding. He and his wife had a big church ceremony, and after they exchanged their vows in front of three hundred people, they thanked the minister and turned to one another to deliver some handcrafted words.

My friend started giving his personal vows to his

bride-to-be. They were sweet, heartfelt, and even funny. "Baby, I love you so much," he said, "I want to vow to you that I'm going to help you every day around the house."

Other people chuckled when he said that, but I actually got a little nervous for the guy. I couldn't believe it—he'd just made a vow in front of three hundred people to help out around the house. Even worse, he tied it directly to how much he loved his new bride. Wouldn't it be better to, in the words of Nike, *just do it*—without calling attention to the act? Now, if he failed to help out around the house, he was breaking his marriage vows.

Well, wouldn't you know it: six months after this couple was married, they ended up in a counselor's office.

They were sitting on the therapy couch when my friend's wife turned to him and said, "You know something? You don't love me."

My friend was astonished. "What do you mean I don't love you? You don't love me!"

"You promised to help me around the house," she said.

To which he replied, "I do help you around the house!"

How could they possibly have misunderstood each other so severely? I'll tell you how: they didn't realize their backgrounds had completely shaped their points of view—and in completely opposite ways.

When my friend was growing up, he saw his father come home at night, tired after a long day of work, and his mother say to him, "Honey, you've slaved away all day. I don't want you to do anything. I want you to sit down in this chair so you can read the paper. I'll bring your favorite drink. And don't worry about anything—I've made the meal. I'll set the table. I'll clean up. I'll put the leftovers away. I'll do the dishes. I'll make sure the laundry's done. I'm gonna do all the work because you've done everything this whole week. You pay our mortgage, and you pay for our cars. You work so hard, and you deserve to rest."

My friend's dad would say, "Baby, let me at least do something to help you."

"I'll have none of it," his wife would say. "You just relax."

"Please, can I help somehow?"

And finally, she would relent. "Okay, honey. Why don't you take the garbage out every night?"

So every night, my friend's dad would take the garbage out. That's what this little boy saw, the same little boy who grew up into a man and got married. When he said, "I'll help around the house," the picture that came to mind was of his dad taking out the garbage. And he did exactly that: he took the garbage out every night.

But what about his wife? When she was growing up, here's what she saw. Her dad would come home and say to her mom, "Baby, you've worked all day just like me. Now I want you to sit down. I know you've prepared the meal, but I'm gonna set the table. I'll clear the table off. I'll put the food back in the refrigerator. I'll do the dishes. I'll make sure the laundry's done. I'll mop up. I'll clean. I want to do everything I can because you've slaved away all day, and I want to really help you around the house. And honey, you sit down here while I get you a dessert. Matter of fact, you can have two desserts. You can have five desserts. I don't care how fat you get 'cause I love you. It doesn't matter. I want to serve you."

That was what this little girl saw, the same little girl who grew up into a woman and married my friend. When she heard, "I'll help around the house," the picture that came to mind was of her dad doing just about everything.

Twenty years later, they found themselves at the altar. When my friend vowed "I'm gonna help you around the house," it meant something entirely different to him than it did to his wife.

So who's right and who's wrong? Well, they're both right. They both had vastly disparate mental images, because of their different upbringings and backgrounds. He saw one thing; she saw something totally different.

When we communicate with each other, we say words that generate a specific picture in our mind's eye. When we have problems understanding one another, it's often because my picture is totally different than yours. You're seeing things based on your background and life experience; I'm seeing things based on mine. We may not be seeing the same thing at all.

We have to be mindful of the words we use, but, more importantly, we have to remember that the same words used by two different people can have vastly different meanings. The more we can explain what we mean, the better shot we have at communicating well. But we also have to be willing to "take out the trash" of our own preconceived notions and mental images. If you want to have good communication, check your baggage at the door. Break the habit of thinking the way it is for you is the way it is for everyone. If you can be open to the mental images *other* people have, it will revolutionize your communication and transform your relationships.

So, baby, will you just take out the trash?

27

TWO GUYS WALK ONTO A PLANE

How much pain do we experience when we try to love someone who refuses to love us back?

We're trying so hard to do the right thing, and yet the people in our lives still reject us. I'll tell you right now: it's incredibly painful. God tells us to love others as we love ourselves, and maybe we do a good job of it—but then we feel angry and wounded when they don't show us the same love in return.

I was flying back from Munich one time, and got waylaid in Chicago. What was supposed to be a brief layover turned out to be not so brief—my flight to Dallas was delayed, so I sat around the airport for three hours, feeling jet-lagged. When our plane was finally ready for boarding, I was happy to plunk myself down into my seat.

The seat next to me was empty, but not for long. A big ol' boy came tromping down the aisle. This guy was probably five-foot-eight and must have weighed 300 pounds. He sat down beside me.

Now, truth be told, I had seen him in the lounge before we boarded. When I looked at him, my first thought was, "Mike, do not judge this man. God loves this guy." That was honestly the first thing that went through my head—his size doesn't matter in the slightest. God loves him, and so will I.

So then he sits down right beside me, and I'm thinking, "Perfect. Now I've got the opportunity to love this guy like God would, to treat him like a human being." So I stuck out my hand and said, "Hey. How are ya?"

No response.

I tried again. I said, "Hi. How are you today, my friend?"

"I heard you the first time," he snapped. He still wouldn't take my hand.

"Oh, okay," I said. "My name's Mike. What's yours?"

He wouldn't even look at me. "No. I'm not doing that." Then he buried himself in his *SkyMall*, making it very obvious the conversation was over.

But it wasn't over for me. "So you're not friendly?" I asked, hoping to find some point of connection.

He still hadn't looked at me, not once. "Nope," he said.

And that was it.

For the next forty-five minutes, our interaction was all I could think about. The guy wouldn't even shake my hand. That's never happened to me before, to have someone so blatantly refuse to acknowledge my humanity.

I tried to distract myself by reading over the notes I'd brought onto the plane with me—I was studying for my WSET (wine snob) diploma—but all I could think was, "What just happened?"

I love people, and I'm a people pleaser. If somebody rejects me and I don't know why, it hurts my feelings. It really hurt that another human being was rejecting me. The little boy in me wanted to engage, and this man had shut me down. The kid inside me felt deeply wounded. And, like most of us when we get wounded, our knee-jerk reaction is fight or flight.

I chose fight. I got angry. I slid open the window shade, telling myself I needed the light so I could see what I was reading. But the guy beside me was watching movies on his computer, and what I really wanted was for the sun beating through the window to create such a strong glare that he wouldn't be able to see his screen. I wanted to hurt him because he'd hurt me. Mostly, I wanted him to be forced to ask, "Hey, could you close the window?" so that I could say, "You didn't choose the window seat, did you?" and snub him back.

That's what was going on inside of me—I felt hurt, angry, and punitive. But I knew I was in the wrong. I thought, "This guy needs to watch his movie." So I didn't say anything and just slid the shade back down. I put my reading light on so I could keep reading.

Yeah, the guy hurt me. But plotting my revenge was just my way of protecting myself. The far greater challenge was to simply love this guy, no strings attached.

What was going on inside of me that I needed this guy's approval? The more I thought about it, the more I saw it as an invitation to intimacy between me—the little boy inside me and the adult boy I am now—and God. Sure, the guy beside me wasn't interested in connecting. But it gave me an opportunity to be intimate with someone else: my Father in heaven.

The Lord showed me something else, too. People watch other people constantly. We watch how people walk, how they dress, how they carry themselves, and the way they treat other people. If I remind somebody of a guy they don't like, they're not going to like me. It ain't about me.

I don't know why the guy sitting beside me didn't like me. But what I realized was that it wasn't about me. Maybe I did something in the lounge that he didn't like. Maybe he didn't like the way I was dressed, in my blue silk shirt and tight jeans. Maybe my man purse really offended him. Or maybe he saw me on my phone and thought, "What an egotistical, eccentric, arrogant prick."

Of course a part of me—the little boy part—wanted to say, "Hey, bro—did I do something to you?" I was still desperately craving approval and acceptance, manically trying to figure out what I did wrong. Eventually, I realized the best thing was to just sit in the discomfort—to sit in those feelings and realize, "It's not about me. So what can I learn from it?"

You can't control the way people feel about you. All you can do is be kind and loving. You can't walk on pins and needles, but you can be cognizant of the world around you—whether that world is an airport, a coffee shop, or the office where you work. The goal is to love the people in front of you the best you can, even when—*especially* when—they're not inclined to love you back.

I have friends who feel disgusted when they have to sit next to a big guy (or lady) on a plane. They're spilling over into your seat, dropping crumbs everywhere. I could have made the choice to judge the guy sitting next to me, decide he was repulsive, and turn my back on him. But I loved him so much that I wanted to connect with him. God put it in my heart to love that man, to give him my care and attention—I figure that's why God sat him next to me in the first place—and then the guy just wouldn't play ball.

In Romans 12:18, the Apostle Paul says, "If possible, so far as it depends on you, be at peace with all men." Emphasis on, *so far as it depends on you.* There are times you simply can't be at peace with all men. But that's okay. You can still love them, just like I tried to do with the guy on the plane.

As we disembarked, I had the urge to tap him on the shoulder and say, "Hey, if I did something to bother you, I apologize. I just want you to know I'm sorry." But I didn't because that still would have been about me—trying to figure out what I did wrong and why he didn't like me.

So I kept walking and kept my mouth shut. Sometimes that's all you can do: love with an open heart and a closed mouth.

But it is still hard, isn't it? Has this ever happened in your life?

28

WHAT THE DISABLED KIDS TAUGHT ME

Who was the last person who taught you about humility and forgiveness? What did they look like? Were they old or young, big or small?

One of the most powerful lessons for me came from an unexpected teacher—not an old sage or a spiritual leader or an academic with three PhDs. No. The best lesson I've ever been taught on humility and forgiveness came from a bunch of disabled kids.

My buddy Greg had invited me to speak at a gala called "Night of the Superstars." It was a sold-out red carpet event like the Academy Awards, but instead of celebrating Tom Cruise, the superstars were disabled kids. Some couldn't walk, some had spina bifida, some couldn't speak or hear, and most were in wheelchairs. That night, it didn't matter what physical challenges these kids had, because each and every one of them was treated like a celebrity.

Thousands of fans lined the auditorium, shouting the kids' names and cheering as they made their way down the aisle. The guests held out their programs for autographs, and the kids did their best to sign their names and pose for pictures with their fans.

But I wasn't there to speak to the kids. Greg had asked me to do a presentation for the adults. He wanted me to explain to the community and the sponsors what he and the organization were doing with these kids. In standing there and observing them, it quickly became clear that I had more to learn than I had to teach. When I got up to speak, my focus was clear.

"You know, we've all probably run into somebody who was born blind," I said. "What you realize is that because of that disability, the other areas of their life are magnified. So for most of them, their sense of hearing is like ten times as good as the average person's. Or their sense of touch, whatever it is. So what can we learn from these kids? What in them is magnified by what we can see that would affect us as men and women today? What can these children teach *us*?"

For me, the glaring attribute that was magnified in their lives was humility. And I'm not talking about humility like, "Woe is me. Everybody's better than me. I'm no good." For these kids, just being outside and existing in the public eye demonstrated their magnified sense of humility. Living in the world became a daily exercise because they constantly encountered people pointing at them, whispering about them, and even laughing at them. Most of these kids had learned at a very young age that the stares, snickers, and pointing had nothing to do with them and everything to do with the discomfort of the people around them.

For the rest of us who don't have easily identifiable disabilities, who don't walk around looking different, we can show our humility by taking an interest in the other human beings that surround us; by showing genuine concern for our bosses, our colleagues and our clients, and asking them what makes them tick; and by really listening when they answer. Being humble is a way of saying, "I'm not the most important person here. *You* are."

The word "humility" is so often misused. Most of the time, when we think of humility, we think of weakness. But I think the world is starting to see a real change in that word.

The biggest place I see that change is with athletes. Take two of the top soccer players in the world. One says, "I'm just very grateful for the gift God has given me, and I'm grateful to my family, too, for helping me grow and develop and get to where I am today." The other soccer player says, "I'm the best there is, man. There's nobody as good as I am."

Why do we want the second guy to fail but the first guy to win? Because the first guy has *humility*.

We can be strong, we can be competitive, and we can be fiercely good at what we do—and we can still be humble. Humility is the ability to step outside of ourselves and actually take an interest in another human being. If I'm a humble person, it means having a concern for someone other than myself.

Who was the strongest man ever to walk on planet Earth? Jesus Christ. Would you consider Him a weakling? No way! He was a man's man. A carpenter. But He acted out of humility. He said, "I'm here to help other people. That's my job." And He did it in a tremendous way.

Humility is the ability to be strong internally—which means looking beyond your own needs and desires. When you have a genuine concern for someone else, and when you help that person get to a level in his or her own life that he or she never would have gotten to without you, you have great inner fortitude. That is strength, not weakness. And that, to me, is true humility.

What else can these kids teach us? Forgiveness. They have no problem forgiving. Not a single one of the superstars I met held a grudge or had a bad word to say about anyone. They were kind and loving toward their parents, siblings, doctors, and friends. They were even forgiving toward the people who were unkind to them—the other kids at school and on the playground who were cruel. They just embodied this incredible air of forgiveness, of trying to meet other people where they were.

How about us? Most of us walk around with three attorneys' numbers in our pockets and figure we'll offer forgiveness after the court case! I think we need to try to understand the way other people are hardwired. If I'm an extrovert and you're an introvert, we may have a lot of misunderstandings. It's the same thing with thinkers versus feelers. But if we take a minute to understand the nature of the people around us, we won't have to waste time getting hurt over differences in our personalities.

And when we do get hurt or offended, we need to learn how to forgive. The word "forgiven" is often associated with religion, but I want to break that association and think about how we can forgive the people around us—and ourselves. How do I forgive myself for the standards I've set for myself that I can't meet? How do I forgive other people when they don't live up to the standards I've set for them?

I've found that 90 percent of offenses can be let go if we sit down at the table together. When I listen to what you have to say with understanding, I'm taking the time to get to know you and figure out "the why" behind "the what," which is what really matters. If we can take the time to find out "the why," we can have communication. We can get to know each other. And after that, forgiving isn't so hard. Neither is saying "I'm sorry," especially in business, where apologies are hard to come by.

What would it look like to live life like these children from the "Night of the Superstars" who magnify humility and forgiveness? And how do we commit ourselves to walking this out in our relationships at home, at church, and in the marketplace?

We can learn so much from these children—from all children—because they're real. They don't have editing facilities. They tell you what they see. Their parents try to instill an editing system in them because of their own fears, and their own sense of embarrassment, but they shouldn't. There's nothing more honest than watching kids interact. And it reminds us that we were all kids once. If we tap into our younger selves and let the child inside of us escape—if we turn off our editing facilities once in a while—we can start relating to other people in a genuine way. We can live like these superstars every day.

Those kids weren't "disabled," at least not in my eyes. They were some of the most wise and able souls I've ever met.

Look at your strengths. What disability has magnified them to make you who you are today?

Part VIII

COVERING OR EXPOSING

29

DON'T WAIT FOR THE FUNERAL
TO EULOGIZE SOMEONE

I love funerals.

Don't get me wrong—I don't love when people die. But I love hearing what people *say* at funerals. They talk about the deceased like he was a hero, a warrior, or a demigod. They talk about all the magnificent things he did and the rich life he lived. They talk about all the people he loved, and the people who loved him, and the funny stories and memories and millions of tiny ways he made life better for everyone else.

The sad thing is that none of those compliments were given to the guy when he was still alive. I wish we could get fifty people into a man's office to say, "Take the afternoon off. Tell your boss that you're not doing any work because we're going to eulogize you right now. We're not waiting twenty years for you to be in a wood box before we do it!"

Why withhold the good stuff until it's too late for the person to enjoy it? Consider this proverb: "Don't withhold good from those to whom it is due when it is in your power to do it."

So if it's in my power to find something good in you, why can't I do that? That takes humility on my part and not saying, "Oh, this guy thinks he's better than me. Oh, this guy, I don't like the way he parts his hair. If I'm nice to him, it's gonna cost me. I gotta be one up on him."

What if we dropped all that kind of thinking and actually took the time to tell people why they're great?

A prophet speaking for God once said, "If you can extract the precious from the vile, then you can be my spokesperson."

Wow. The precious from the vile—that sounds pretty intense. The problem is we're all really well-versed in seeing the vile. Sometimes, when we look at our spouses or our close friends, it's all we see. We swim in it.

Just spend enough time with anyone, and you'll see something that you don't like. And after a while, *that's all you'll see.* Whatever negative qualities I see in you, I'm going to look for. And when I'm looking, I'll find them. Once I find them, I'm going to judge you for them. It all starts with a belief on my part.

But what if I could learn to eulogize the living and find ways to encourage people to be the best versions of themselves? What if that were our goal in life?

Let's say you see a woman at a restaurant with an autistic child, and the kid is howling, really letting loose. Your gut reaction might be to think, "Ugh. Why can't that woman control her kid?"

But then you take a breath and step back from your initial instinct. You notice how gently she is speaking to her son, how patiently she's cutting up his steak into bite-sized nibbles. She isn't yelling back at him; she is calmly reassuring him, speaking softly with love and kindness, until his own temper tantrum fades, and he begins quietly eating his meat.

After your meal, you go up to the table. "Excuse me, ma'am," you say. "I'm sorry, I don't mean to interrupt you—but I just love the way you love your boy. That interaction I saw just now was really cool."

Tears spring to her eyes. "Thank you," she says. "You don't know how many dirty looks I get from diners who wish my son would 'just shut up.' So many people are angry with us when we go out to eat that sometimes we're afraid to go out to restaurants at all. I can't tell you how much it means to me, what you said."

I guarantee both you *and* that woman are going to

be on cloud nine for the rest of the day.

What if we constantly looked for ways to encourage people? What if we ignored our knee-jerk reaction to criticize, belittle, and complain, and instead looked for opportunities to offer up little bite-sized eulogies every day?

I want to be known as the guy who encourages. I want people to say, "Whatever you're doing, this guy's going to encourage you, man. You're just going to want to be around him because he's going to motivate you, he's going to coach you, and he's going to push you. He's not going to push you into doing things wrong, but he's going to find out what you do well and push you to a higher level—outside *and* inside."

We can work on the exterior, but it's the interior—the heart—that's most significant. Be your own interior designer. What style would you promote?

Look at a house. What's the first thing you notice when you walk in? The floors? Wow, hardwood. Granite countertops. Nice furniture. But here's what people don't pay attention to: there's an HVAC system that heats and cools your home. Is it a good one? Will it break in a year? Nobody looks for the things you can't see. Electrical, lighting, plumbing—the things you don't see are the most important parts of a home. It's the same with our own bodies; it's our internal organs that make our bodies function. Without the interior, there is no exterior.

What if we actually encouraged the internal, the *character* that we see in others? What if we focused on acknowledging and lauding the *courage* in our friends? The *joy* in our coworkers? The *love* in the strangers we cross paths with? The *passion* in our kids? The *commitment* in our spouses?

That takes looking out from ourselves at someone else, taking focus off of ourselves onto someone else. Being observant ("servant" is in this word) of others, looking for ways to encourage based on what we see. Now that is a sport at which I would like to be a professional: seeing the why behind the what, so I can help others reach their full potential. Being a professional encourager without compensation? That's from the heart. Not that professional coaches shouldn't get paid, but if we all were like this? Everyone needs to be coached and encouraged.

What would be a better response you would like to hear about yourself? You go to dinner with a person, and after dinner they report back to their friends. When asked how the night was, what is their response? "Wow, *that* person is the most interesting person I have ever met" or "That person told me that *I* am the most interesting person they have ever met"? One focuses on you, the other on them. It just takes a small shift in our thinking. But that small shift will ultimately make a *huge* change in us.

Watch how people will *want* to be around you. Your influence will increase by a very small shift in thinking. If a Boeing 777 leaves New York headed for Japan, and it is just a few degrees off? No telling where the plane will end up—Alaska? Small shifts produce huge changes.

You may end up receiving the rarest—yet most sought-after—compliment. The best compliment that you could ever give another person is that you like yourself when you are with him or her. This statement says so much about that person. When you like yourself most, who are you with?

30

THE PEA-HEAD AT STARBUCKS

How often do you pass judgment on someone you just met, maybe someone you've never even talked to?

I'll tell you how often: *every single day.*

We all do it—as humans, we're trained to judge. Every day, hour, and minute of our lives, we pass judgments on people because of the way they look or the clothes they wear. We might even judge them based on their skin color, shape, hairstyle, or tattoos.

"Not me, Mike," you say. "I don't judge." Trust me—you do. You do it constantly, and worse than that, you do it unconsciously. Most times, you probably don't even know you're doing it.

The same goes for me.

A couple of months ago, I walked into a Starbucks

and stood behind a guy who was six-foot-four and a weightlifter. He was huge. You could land an airplane on his back. His legs were as big as my waist. His arms were the size of my thighs. But he had a tiny little pea-head. And I thought to myself, "This guy's got an IQ of about 48. You know—the IQ of an average-sized garden pea."

Then he hopped up to the counter and said, in this very warm and intelligent voice, "Hi, good morning. I would like a decaf latte, non-foam, and put some extra sugar in it, please." And I looked at him, shocked to hear the voice that was so incongruous with the body in front of me.

Here I was, judging the guy, assuming he's got three words in his vocabulary and two of them are "uh," based on what I saw from a distance. What did I know?

Turns out that the guy and I were on the same latte schedule. Every weekday at three o'clock, boom, there we were in Starbucks, standing next to each other in line. I chatted him up—because that's what I do—and it turned out he was a Rhodes Scholar. He has a PhD in nutrition and is one of the most articulate men I've ever met.

Man, was I wrong about him. And I'm going to go out on a limb here and say you're probably wrong, too, when you judge random strangers. That's the thing about judgment: it's rarely based in truth.

What would life be like if we took the time to get to know people and stopped judging them based on their skin color, sexual preference, hair color, height, or job? How many more people would we get close to if we actually took a genuine interest in *who they are*, humbled ourselves, and left judgment at the door?

Who knows, we might even save lives. Let's say there's a guy in the near distance who's grabbing a woman by her neck. He's got a knife, and it looks like he's about to stab her. Now imagine I happen to have a gun with me and I'm a sharpshooter. I pull the gun out, and I aim it because I believe this woman's on the verge of death. I think I'm going to save her life. So I shoot. I hit him. He dies.

But the woman dies too. What if I didn't realize that he was a physician and she was choking to death and he was trying to save her with an emergency tracheotomy? I made a snap judgment, and now it's too late. They're both dead.

I won't lie to you. It takes serious time and effort to break the pattern of judging. We act like passing judgment is our birthright, our second skin. But like most things, you start small.

It took me all of ten seconds to realize the pea-head at Starbucks was anything but. Turns out, *I* was the pea-head for making such an ignorant assumption!

So how then do we *not* judge? Is it just a matter of willpower? Do we just decide not to judge and, boom, we don't? Is it something we have *some* control over, or is it like the weather, something we can never control?

Why is it that we have understanding and compassion when others have the same faults as we do or have experienced the same things as we have, but when their faults are foreign to us or their life experiences are different, we judge them? Before it happened to me, I used to pity people that went through a divorce. Now I understand and sympathize with them. Why? We share a fraternity now.

Consider, then, that in actuality, we all share the same exact life experiences. We are all human, all have skin, and all are valued equally. We all had parents, and we all walk on planet Earth. Sure, we can narrow down and talk about things like how your childhood was worse or better than mine, you had more or less money, or your education was better or worse; or if you are healthier than me or not, you are better looking or not, or you are more privileged or not. You get the picture. What is most important is that we realize that we may be different outwardly, but we are the same inwardly, both physically—with lungs, kidneys, a heart, a brain—and emotionally—with thoughts, feelings and a spirit.

It is as simple as putting yourself on "pause" and "pressing play" on the other person. Just understand that there are more people around you that need to hear from you. "Thank you. You are very good. I am sorry; did I interrupt? Please forgive me." At times, this takes just simple humility, putting your ego aside.

It is a humbleness to understand that *you* are one of seven billion people on planet Earth, with a lot of sameness. Sure, do your best, take advantage of what life is offering, but understand that behind it all is *one* that is much larger than *you*, and this one has a purpose for *you* that is larger than the world you presently live in.

How do you start? Next time you are at a restaurant, shopping mall, Starbucks, wherever there is a crowd, observe. Who don't you like? Why?

Figure out a way to meet these people and encourage them, and see what happens.

Will you at least try this once in the next week?

31

TEACH YOUR KIDS BY EXAMPLE

I have a buddy in LA who's going through a rough patch in his marriage. He and his wife fight a lot, but he's the kind of guy who, after five minutes in an argument, says, "I've had enough. I'm out." And then he leaves the house before things escalate.

"I have to do it like that, Mike," he told me. "I don't want our kids to see it. I want to protect them as much as I can from when Liz and I fight."

"I understand, my friend," I told him. "But your kids see more than you realize. They already know what's going on."

He has a ten-year-old son and a seven-year-old daughter, and both of his kids are angry. They don't know *why* they're angry, but believe me, they are.

Now, keep in mind these are great people. My friend, his wife, their two kids—they're all decent folks. But when my buddy and his wife are together, it's toxic. To his credit, he is trying to figure out what he needs to do to make the situation palatable, what he can work on for the whole relationship to change.

The thing is, they think they're hiding it from their kids, but they're not. The other day my buddy sat down with his elder child and said, "Son, Mom and I are having a tough time right now."

And his son said, "*Right now*, Dad? We saw that years ago!"

This kid is ten years old, and he's seen everything. We think we're hiding stuff, but other people see it, especially our kids. They see a whole lot more than we realize, and they are more attuned to the emotional truths of our lives than just about anyone else.

It's only natural that, if we have children, we feel a responsibility to help them read Scripture and grow up with an understanding of who God is. No doubt about that. And I know many good Christian men and women who take their kids to Sunday school religiously every week, never missing a Sunday. But I think the bigger teaching lesson is this: those kids are looking at *us*. Our children look at us as role models, and they will copy the behavior we model for them. That's worth a hundred lessons in Sunday school.

My buddy's kids sit in those tiny plastic chairs every Sunday, but is that really where they're getting their spiritual meat for the week? "Sure, I'll read the Bible, Mom and Dad," they say, "because you tell us this is what we need to be doing. But are you walking this out? We watch you every day, and we know when you're fighting and when you won't speak to each other, and we don't see you living God's truth in your day-to-day lives. So why should *we* do it?"

Kids are smart. They know more about you than you think, and they know when you're walking the walk and when you're not. They can tell.

So what *are* God's truths? And how do we live them out every day, modeling for our kids the lives Christ wants us to have?

Here are three truths I believe all parents should try to get across to their children.

Truth number one: *Jesus died on the cross for our sins.* That's a gift. Eternal life is a gift. You just need to, in faith, say, "Lord, I believe what you did for me." It's a confession of faith, and then, boom, you're starting at the finish line.

Truth number two: *Feel your own feelings.* We have to teach our children how to feel their own feelings. Why are you feeling the way you are? Because every time my buddy walks out on his wife and slams the door behind them, he's teaching his kids not to feel. He's teaching his ten-year-old son that it's okay to leave when things get tough, to bottle up his own emotions and block out the people who love him. He's teaching his seven-year-old daughter that it's okay to be in a relationship with a man who won't be emotionally open and vulnerable with her.

We have to teach our children at a young age not to blame. "Well, if this ..." "If what?" "Well, if he didn't ..." "Well, okay. He did." "Yeah, well, if he didn't then I wouldn't feel ..."

Those are the sorts of things we hear from our kids when they're small—but aren't they also the same list of excuses we make for our husbands, our wives, our parents, our coworkers? Some of us really never do grow up!

I say no. That language has to go, whether you're eight or forty-eight. You feel what you're feeling, so own up to those emotions. It's not about him, or her, or anybody but you. You could have felt something different. Somebody else could be put in the same situation and have a totally different feeling. So own your feelings. Make a decision. Make it *your* decision and stand by it.

That's truth number three: *Make a decision and stand by it.* We have to teach our kids how to feel, but we also have to help them understand that their feelings don't always align with the truth. The truth is what God says, not how we feel. Our emotions are indicators of what we believe. That's all a feeling is. And all you can do is make the best decision you can with the information you have—based on God's truth—and then stand by that decision.

When your kids make decisions, you want to be the first one by their side, saying, "That was a good decision." Even when they're saying to you, "But Dad, I failed."

That's when you tell them, "It was a great decision, because at the time that was all the information you had. You didn't know what the outcome was going to be, but you owned your feelings, made a decision, and stood by the outcome. That takes character and strength."

If you can instill that wisdom in your kids when they're young, they will grow up with a sense of how to make choices in life. "I get to feel my own feelings," they'll say, "and see what's going on, and then when I make a decision, I own it. And I know when I make a decision, it's a good decision."

A lot of kids grow up being told constantly that their decisions are wrong. "Why'd you do that?" my dad used to say to me, after I did anything, from big stuff to small stuff. I got that for many, many, many years. Even as an adult, it was really hard to make a decision, because I was never sure if it was the right one. To this day I still second-guess myself. Why? Because I still hear my dad's voice in my head, saying,

"What if it's wrong? What if it's not good?"

Teach your kids the three truths, and model those truths by example. *Accept Jesus into your heart. Feel your own feelings. Make decisions and stand by them.* Encourage your kids in the area of decision-making, because it will serve them well for the rest of their lives. And that's the sort of lesson they're going to learn at home, not at some school. Formal education only takes your kids so far. It's up to you to teach them at home, because that's where they're really watching, listening, learning—and trying to be like you.

They may hear it at church, listen to it from you, but learn it as they observe you. Fact is, kids have no one else to observe but their parents. But who do the parents observe?

32

TAKE IT UP WITH YOUR DADDY

A few years ago, I was part of a church that was studying *The Purpose Driven Life*. Rick Warren's book was super popular at the time, and still is—it's the best-selling hardcover non-fiction book in history and the second-most translated book in the world, after the Bible.

So this church would break down into small groups hosted by different families. There were usually about fifteen people per home, and they'd go through a chapter a week.

One day after church, a man came up to the pastor and said, "We'd like to study *The Purpose Driven Life*, too. Could you have somebody come and teach it to us?"

"Sure," said the pastor.

Then the man explained there were eight of them, four couples—and they were all homosexuals.

No one would teach them. The pastor went from person to person, asking different teachers in the church community, and everybody said no.

But the pastor didn't give up. He said, "I think I know somebody who will take that job on." And he came to me and asked if I'd be willing to teach this group.

"I'd be honored," I said. "I'd love to do that."

Now, no one had told me that this group was expecting a "pastor," not a businessman. So I showed up at their house in a pair of jeans, cowboy boots, and a T-shirt, holding a Bible. They took one look at me and said, "You're the minister?"

"Well," I said, "I'm a business guy, and I'm here to lead."

I went in and they had wine and cheese all laid out. I thought to myself, "I could get used to this." But before I started in on the lesson, the man whose house it was asked me a question.

"Before you teach us," he said, "we need to know if you think what we're doing—living a homosexual life—is wrong."

I paused.

"Great question!" I said, "If you want to talk about

right and wrong, let me tell you what I believe. I believe that when a person is confronted with the claims of Jesus of Nazareth being the son of God, who came to planet Earth to be crucified, died, buried, and raised from the dead for the forgiveness of sin—when a person is presented with that truth and they go, 'Nah, not for me,' I believe that person is wrong."

This gentleman nodded, following me so far. I went on. "If a person is presented with that truth and they receive it as a gift and a promise of grace, forgiveness, and mercy from God the Father, and they adopt that for themselves, I believe that person is right."

I had their full attention. I looked this man straight in the eye.

"You are asking me about your behavior. You need to take that up with your heavenly Daddy. I'm here to talk to you about my Savior and my friend Jesus. Get to know Him and He will speak to you about your life choices."

They looked at each other and went, "You can teach us."

And I did.

It wasn't my job to lecture them on their life choices. My job was to bring them closer to my Father. The Holy Spirit is big enough to do in a person's life what the Holy Spirit wants and needs to do. He certainly doesn't need my help or my judgment!

We spend way too much time trying to change people's behavior and not enough time taking an interest in them over a glass of wine! Too much time analyzing what a person is doing and not enough time being in a relationship with them to understand why they are doing it. Too much time criticizing, not enough time loving!

Ask yourself this question: how do you love the unlovable? The answer is found when you find and get to know someone who can't love you.

33

THANK YOU, MOM AND DAD

My dad is Irish; my mom's Italian. What a combo, right? There was so much passion in my house. I was raised Catholic, so I grew up with a basic understanding of God—I knew God sent His son to planet Earth and all that. But I had such a legalistic understanding of the truth. It doesn't mean the *truth* was legalistic, just that my understanding of it was.

When most of us look back at our childhoods, we want to blame our moms and dads. "If my parents hadn't gotten divorced, if they hadn't done *this*, if they hadn't said *that* ... then I wouldn't be where I am today." It's so easy to blame our pasts. And I'm not saying some people haven't been victims. Plenty of men and women have gone through tremendously hard times. But there comes a point in our lives when we have to stop and go, "I'm responsible for how I'm going to respond to the things that happened to me." Even if we weren't responsible for what happened to us as kids, as adults, we are responsible for how we let those events affect us.

When I look back on my own childhood, I get to make a choice. I get to say, "Thank you, Mom and Dad, for what you provided for me. You gave me a home, an upbringing, and an education. You've done a lot for me. You also provided my foundation of Christianity."

Now, sure, that foundation was through the Catholic Church. It was all about, "Are you doing the right thing? You have to do this. You can't do that. You can't eat meat on Friday, and you can't do these twenty things or God's going to punish you." I was constantly afraid of God because I could never do the right thing. Never. I'd always screw up. And then, just when I thought I'd gotten it right, I'd screw up again.

Does it sound like I'm blaming my parents? No. I'm responsible today. As an adult, I get to say, "I learned a lot from my parents, whom I love very much. God bless them. They're both deceased and with the Lord today."

Now, what if I decide my upbringing did me irreparable harm? I say, "I'm going to avoid all the pain and hurt I felt as a child." So I live my whole life determined not to be the way I was—and that avoidance ends up controlling my whole life.

Imagine a big hole in the middle of your street. If your car goes in it, you never see your car again. Naturally, the people on your street are freaked out. Some of them say, "Oh my God, I can't drive down my street." Every time they leave the house they have to drive north instead of south. They won't go near the hole, they won't let their kids near it—they won't even walk within ten feet of it. That hole ends up dictating how they live their lives.

If "the hole" for you is your family background—the way you were raised, the belief systems you grew up with—and you're determined to avoid it at all costs, then it's still controlling you. I don't know about you, but I don't want that to be the way I live. Those things that I thought were negative in my past? I don't want them to control the way I live now. Isn't it better to accept responsibility for the life we have *today*?

When I was twenty years old, I still had a long way to go when it came to letting go of the past and not letting it control me. But I had begun to understand that gratitude was a whole lot better than the alternative. In my senior year of college, I sat down and I wrote my mom and dad the following letter:

> *Hi Mom and Dad,*
> *I certainly haven't forgotten you all. I've been really busy with school, the LSAT, apartment*

hunting, and what have you. Here is an article that appeared in our school's newspaper, The Minaret. I thought you might like to have it. School is fine—no job yet—LSAT Saturday—car still in my possession—understanding God better every day—still broke—still with my girlfriend—still love you, mom and dad—still wondering how everything is doing—still love Dannon yogurt—still exercising—and on top of all this, I'm happy.

Dad: I'm happy because I've finally realized what you and mom have done for me over the years. You helped me go to school in Tampa—I always had a beautiful room and house to stay in—I always ate extremely well—when I needed money you gave it to me. When I made too many phone calls, long distance, you talked to me about it, but still understood and took care of it. Dad, I realize everything you have done for me, and I love you for it. Words can't describe how I feel—just thank you.

See you all later.

Love, Mike

Four years later, that dream *had* become a reality. After I got out of school, I wrote to my dad again. This time I sent him the following letter:

Dad,

Some thoughts that keep me going:

I want to diminish my need to be liked and strengthen my need to be respected.

I want to stop comparing myself to my peers and start comparing myself to myself.

I want to outgrow my childish instinct to bear a grudge.

I want to make sure my parents know how much I love them.

Instead of worrying about turning 30, then 40, then 50, I want to celebrate the fact that I was born at all.

I want to see the big picture, to realize that I am one of 237 million people in this country (which is only one of 180 countries on this earth). That means I should not think more highly of myself than what God intended for me.

I want to continuously realize that Jesus is my only salvation.

Thought these might interest you!

- M

A decade earlier, I would never, not in a million years, have sent my dad a letter like that. I was angry with my family, not grateful for them. I was not a very thankful human being in general. I was still driving around the hole in the street, ordering my whole life around my negative association with the past.

But what if we faced that hole and filled it with gratitude? What if *you* wrote a letter, not an email, *a letter,* to the people you were once angry with, or disappointed in, and instead of raking them over the coals, you thanked them instead?

Part IX

KIND OF A SUPERHERO

34

THE IRON CROSS

Sometimes young guys come up to me and ask me about my workout routine. "Are you into weightlifting?" they ask.

"Yeah, I'm into weightlifting."

They always give me a sideways look. "But you don't go to the gym."

"You can be into weightlifting and not go to the gym."

"What do you mean?"

"You can help lift the weights off the shoulders of the people you walk with, the people who are bound down and don't understand the God of love, mercy, and grace. You can help lift the weights off their shoulders by speaking the truth. And you can do that by knowing the truth yourself and being so grounded in it that you become a serious, true weightlifter."

That's the kind of weightlifting I do. And I don't even break a sweat!

Where is your weightlifting done? At home? The marketplace? The gym?

When I was growing up, I loved watching the gymnasts in the Olympics. I wanted more than anything to be one. They were all ripped and buffed out, and I thought being a gymnast would be the coolest thing.

But like most kids growing up, I played baseball and basketball. My parents wouldn't let me play football because they didn't want me to get hurt. Go figure. But when I got into high school, I started lifting weights. When I got into college, I decided to make good on that childhood dream of being a gymnast. I took a phys ed class and told the coach, "I'm going to try out for the gymnastics team."

"Great," the coach said. "What school did you do it in?"

"I've never done it before," I said. "But I've been in your phys ed class here, and I know I can do it."

"Mike," he said, "it's impossible. There's no way you're going to make the gymnastics team. These guys have been doing this since they were five years old."

But I was committed. "Can you at least give me a shot?"

"Sure, I'll give you a shot," he said and kind of

laughed.

Here's what he didn't know. I was determined. I was taking a full load at school, but I practiced and worked out *six hours a day*. Not five hours, not five hours and forty-five minutes. If I didn't hit six hours during the day, I'd go to the gym at eleven o'clock at night so I got my six hours in. And I didn't do it five days a week. I did it seven.

Over and over and over again I practiced. I didn't stop. I committed fully to it—and then I tried out for the coach's gymnastics team.

My crowning moment was when I did the Iron Cross. It's a move you do on the rings, and it takes a killer amount of upper body strength. You basically extend both arms straight out from the sides of your body while suspended mid air for at least two seconds. It's incredibly hard.

So there I was, my hands on the rings, my body extended in a cross, sweat pouring off me. And right in that moment I got to thinking about Jesus Christ. In those two seconds, I realized something about the God of the universe. I was in college, remember, still thinking of God in the same legalistic way I had as a kid. And I thought to myself, "The God I'm used to is going to punish me if I screw up. If I do something wrong and fall off the rings and get into some kind of accident, it'll be my fault because I probably did something to deserve it. But if God is really a God of love and mercy and grace; and He wants to take all my sins—past, present, and future; and He wants to give me a future and a hope; and He's for me and not against me; well, then that's a very different God than the God I'm used to. That's the kind of God I'd like to know. And I'm determined to find out if that's the truth or not."

In the same way I was determined to make the gymnastics team, I was determined to find God's truth.

What happened after my gymnastics tryouts? I made the team—barely, but I made it.

That day on the Iron Cross really set me in motion. It was a trait I'd learned in sports: utter and total determination. I had an attitude of, "I will commit to this 100 percent, because I've gotta find out."

That day was the first day in a long journey, one that has taken me to where I am today. But I *did* find God's truth, and the truth is I am a walking, living example that God is who He says He is, a God of mercy and love.

I'm just one person. If God's love is as deep and wide as an ocean, I've only got a shot glass full of it. But that's all it takes. One little shot glass has completely transformed my life—and it can transform yours.

Can it transform yours?

35

GOD HAD THE FIRST TATTOO

Recently, I was at 24-Hour Fitness. I looked to my left and noticed the guy on the machine beside me. He was this huge guy, probably six-foot-four, in really good shape. I'm talking solid muscle—certainly in better shape than I'll ever be. From the neck down, every inch of his body was covered in tattoos. He had so many tattoos I couldn't even see his skin.

"Dude," I said. "I love your tattoos."

He looked at me, angry and a little bit suspicious. "What?"

"I just want to say I really like your tattoos."

"Whatever, man," he said. He thought I was messing with him.

"I'm serious," I said. "Can I share something with you? Do you know who the first person was to ever have tattoos?"

He still looked suspicious, but now he looked a little curious, too. "You mean like the founder of tattoos?"

"You could say that," I said.

"No. Who?"

I smiled. "God."

He half smiled back. He was probably thinking, "Who is this crazy God man, and could I take him in a fight?" (The answer was yes, he could definitely take me in a fight. It'd be like a modern-day David and Goliath, only without the slingshot or the glory.)

"You think I'm lying to you?" I said. "In the Book of Isaiah God says, 'Behold, I have inscribed you on the palms of My hands.'" I slapped this big guy on the back. "That means, if you believe in the One who made you through His Son, God has you inscribed on the palms of His hands. He had a tattoo long before you did—with your name on it."

This guy looked kind of astonished—maybe even grateful. I figured he was used to his tattoos getting a very different reaction: mothers in supermarkets saying, "Oh my God!" and clutching their little kids closer to them, or people crossing to the other side of the street so they wouldn't have to walk within fifteen feet of this guy.

"Don't let anybody judge you for those tattoos," I told him. "Dude, wear 'em as a badge of honor. Because when you're one of God's children, those tattoos become His. I see you've got a nose ring, too. Did you know Jesus had the first body piercing on the planet?"

Now this guy was really getting a kick out of my little impromptu sermon. He raised an eyebrow. "*Really.*"

"Sure. He got some mighty big holes in His feet and hands, from hanging on that cross! So don't let anybody get down on you because you've got a nose ring."

Wouldn't you know it? This guy stopped working out. He got off his machine, and he and I actually sat down together and had a real conversation, about tattoos and piercings and God's love. I doubt either of us has ever had a conversation quite like it!

I told this story recently at a conference where I was speaking. There were over six hundred businessmen and women in the auditorium, most between the ages of twenty-two and fifty-five. There was a guy in the sixth row who had tattoos all over his body, which definitely stood out in a room of a bunch of businesspeople in suits.

But here's the thing—I had a suspicion that there were a lot more tattoos in that room than just that one guy's. Just because his were more visible didn't mean he was the only one.

"How many people in here have tattoos?" I asked the audience. "Raise your hand if you've got one."

Half the audience tentatively raised their hands. I loved it! "Look," I said, "I don't care why you got the tattoo or where it is on your body. It doesn't matter. God owns 'em, and God loves 'em, because those tattoos are going to become a part of your platform to share His love and goodness with other people. And honestly, if you're sitting in this room, wondering, 'Should I get a tattoo? Is it wrong? Is it right?' then I'm going to tell you right now, go out and do it!"

Half of the audience was sort of giggling, the other half looked shell-shocked. "Good grief," I said, "You think God gets pissed off 'cause you get a tattoo? You don't know the God of the Universe if you really believe that!"

The God of my understanding is not going to excommunicate you because you inked a butterfly on your ankle or a chain on your arm. The God of my understanding loves every inch of you—even the tattoos on your skin. In fact God started the whole trend! He's got you inked on the palms of His hands.

How do you imagine He "scrolled" your name?

36

WHY THE CHURCH NEEDS CROSSFIT

Last week I went to a CrossFit gym. Usually I have a trainer come to my house, but this time I decided to get out and see what the gym was like.

Boy, am I glad I did.

There were about twenty other people working out at the gym, all completing the CrossFit program but working out at their own level. The manager explained to me that these men and women usually come for the same time slot so they've all gotten to know each other, and many of them have become friends. Even if they're working out at their own pace, they're also there as a group, supporting each other and cheering one another on.

So I did my whole circuit—push-ups, burpees, chin-ups, rope climbs, the whole set—and at CrossFit you sometimes end with an outside run. So I did my run, and when I jogged back through the front door of the gym, everybody was cheering me on. People who didn't even know me were giving me high fives and thumbs up all over the place. It felt great.

Everybody else had gotten back from the run, but we were still missing one guy. I'd noticed him earlier—he was a big guy, quite a bit overweight. He was still out there. We were all waiting. People kept craning their necks, staring out the door and looking for this guy. Some of them looked worried. Where was he? Was he going to make it? Would he be okay?

And then finally he came barreling through the door, sweating like you wouldn't believe, and the whole place just erupted into cheers. People were laughing and crying and yelling. The manager told me this guy had never finished before. It was the first time he'd completed the whole circuit, including the run.

I was standing next to two girls who had tears running down their faces, all for this guy they'd been cheering on in class the whole time. I looked at those girls crying and thought, you know what? This is the way church is supposed to be.

I'll take it a step further. I actually found myself thinking, "I'm at church right now."

It was the perfect example of what God intended The Church to be. This is exactly what we Christians ought to be doing—cheering each other on. And when one of us stumbles, the others are there to help pick him up so that he can finish the race.

Maybe you have a brother in Christ who is homosexual (there are a host of people who believe that being gay and Christian are antonyms). Don't judge him. Love him wherever he's at. You're there to support him and be his cheerleader and help him carry his struggles. No judgment, no condemnation. How different is that from someone who passes judgment on a fellow believer? I've known people who lecture their brothers in Christ on how they're not wearing the right tie to church on Easter Sunday. That's not what church is about!

Church is about loving your brothers and sisters in Christ—rejoicing with them when they rejoice, grieving with them when they grieve. I think about those two girls at CrossFit, crying tears of joy because the guy finally finished. That's what I'm talking about when I talk about community. That's what the church needs to be.

I also understand that God has given us a new nature, and that nature will be as He desires. The old is gone. The new has come. God does the changing. We do the loving.

No wonder you don't want to go to church, as long as it's the place where you go to get judged! Why should anyone want to go to a place that reinforces the message that you're always doing, thinking, and feeling the wrong thing? "You're no good. You won't amount to anything. You'll never catch up." Those are the sermons we preach to our brothers and sisters in Christ—and they're the farthest things from God's truth.

Why would I want to subject myself to those messages when I could go to a CrossFit gym and have people encourage me, cheer me on, and think that I'm okay exactly as I am?

Since when did CrossFit become more Christian than the Cross itself?

Here's what I think church should look like. Some guy or girl—not necessarily the pastor—stands up and says, "We're going to have a thirty-minute testimony time, and I'll be the moderator. You each get three minutes, so if you go past four, I'm going to cut you off. Not because we don't like you, but because we want to hear from a lot of people. Come on up and take the mic."

So Ronnie comes on up and takes the mic.

"Man, I'm really struggling with Internet pornography," Ronnie says. "It's ruining my marriage and taking the joy out of everything."

Ronnie takes a deep breath.

"Last week one of my sons found out what I was doing, and he started doing it, too. When I caught him on our home computer, it just about broke my heart. I cried out to God, 'What kind of a father am I being? What kind of example am I setting for my boys as they grow up?' They're just imitating me. As long as I have this addiction, there's a good chance I'll give it to my kids.

"So I need help. I need encouragement. I know it's not who I am. Deep down I know I don't need to be looking at that—I just don't know how to stop."

And then, instead of a bunch of people shaking their heads and looking at the guy with scorn, here's what happens: other people stand up and cheer this guy on.

"It's amazing you shared this with us, Ron," says Suzanne.

"We bless you for it," says Tommy, "and we believe in you."

"Thank you for being so transparent and real and vulnerable with us," adds Liz. "You know we love you, Ronnie."

Compare that to, "You did *what*? That's disgusting. Are you going to therapy? You really should be. Haven't you heard of the filters you can put on your computer to keep you from doing that?"

Which one is more freeing? Which response would *you* rather get from the people who are supposed to be your brothers and sisters?

We have to cheer people on when they make mistakes. That's community. That's what it means to be a family of believers. If you truly believe in what Christ did for us on the Cross, then you've got to share that love CrossFit-style.

We have a lot of single men and women in the world. Which is more freeing: telling a single person that if you have sex before marriage it's a sin and "don't do it!" or a man in a relationship with God saying, "I get to (not have to) protect His daughter and withhold my desires until she becomes my wife or protect her while dating her for her future husband"?

Because someone may be dating your future wife, and you would hope he is protecting her for you!

Which is more freeing?

37

A PIECE OF FLESH

The first tape I ever made was called *Meet the Main Man*. I made about 5,000 copies—sold some and gave some away to friends and family. Once I converted the audio into CD format, I made 50,000 more copies. Those CDs are out in the world somewhere, though I have no way of knowing where.

The other day I got a call from a guy in Portland, Oregon. "I need to speak to Mike Moore," he said. My cell phone hasn't changed since 1993 when I first got my phone number. I've had the same number for twenty-two years.

"This is Mike Moore," I said.

"Are you the Mike Moore who did *Meet the Main Man*?"

"Yup, that's me."

"Mike, I want to let you know that my wife and I

and our two children have listened to your CD five times. We were in the process of a divorce, but we are staying together because of this."

I was shocked. God said to me, "Mike. If all this was just for that one couple, would that have been worth it?"

And my response was, "Yes. Absolutely."

I want to be a change agent in the lives of people. That's all I want. All I care about in life is getting people to change their views of God. When your view of God changes, and you see Him the way He wants to be seen, your whole life changes. Your relationships change, too—your marriage, your relationships with your kids, and your relationships at work. Your view of God will dictate how you walk your life out on this planet.

I have no clue where those 50,000 CDs are in the world, but if they've helped one person, they've done their job. And I've done my job.

I'm not special. It's not like He *chose* me, Mike Moore, to be a conduit of His love. God doesn't trust me. I'm as fickle and untrustworthy as they come! He trusts *Himself* in me. When God speaks through me, it's truly an amazing feeling.

I'm just a piece of flesh, but that's the thing about God: He can take a piece of flesh and do the most miraculous things.

Here's an example. In 2005, I was getting ready to go to Guatemala to speak at a conference with a friend of mine. I was excited about it—Guatemala is beautiful, and I was looking forward to a stimulating conference, great coffee, and some of the nicest people you've ever met.

I was packing my bag, preparing to get on a plane the next day, when my friend and travel buddy called me up. "There's been a mudslide, Mike," he said. "The hotel we were going to stay in got buried."

The 2005 mudslides in Guatemala are some of the worst on record. Over 2,000 people died. If my friend and I had been in that hotel one night earlier, we would have died, too.

When I share this story with a large group, I always ask, "How many times have you been saved from death?" Occasionally people have a story to tell—about the time a tornado struck two blocks away from their house, or how they were supposed to be on American Flight 11 the morning of September 11.

But the truth is we have no idea how many times we've been saved from death. We don't know, because it didn't happen! How many bullets were coming at your head that you didn't even know about because God stopped them? How many traffic accidents? How many tragic cases of being in the wrong place at the wrong time?

God is watching out for us. He is protecting us—even if we don't always know when or how. God already saved us from eternal death by sending His son to die on the cross. But I'm also willing to bet that each of us, over the course of our lives, has been saved from *physical* death dozens, if not hundreds, of times.

So what do we do with that? We have to trust that the one who knows more than us does, in fact, know more than us. We live in this dimension, but God doesn't. God is not in time and space. He wants to walk with us through life, and if we open ourselves to that relationship, it means we depend on Him. We have to believe He can see the future in ways we can't even imagine. And the future God sees for us? It's the best there is.

It has to be; it cost more than the wealth of all nations put together since the beginning of time. It cost more than what it would cost to buy the universe. It was priceless.

Only God could make that payment.

Would you receive a gift that generous from someone? Why not from Him?

Part X

PROTECTING YOUR INVESTMENT

38

WHO YOU ARE IN THIRTY SECONDS

If you had thirty seconds to stand up in front of a group of people right now and tell them who you are, what would you say?

Let's make it even more interesting. Let's say that you have to believe whatever comes out of your mouth about yourself. You can't lie or be selective with the truth. You also can't answer the question of "Who are you?" with "I'm a doctor" or "I teach kindergarten." We don't want to know what you do; we want to know who you *are*.

So, who are you? Are you mean? Kind? Jealous? Are you a brave person? Bitter? Loving? Are you a child of God?

The answer to that last question is, obviously, yes. You are a child of God.

When was the last time you read from the book of

Exodus in the Bible? Exodus is actually a history book. If you read a US history book with Abraham Lincoln in it, no one ever doubts for a second that he was real, because it's solid history. But as soon as people say, "Oh, Exodus is in the *Bible*," people get all weirded out, as though the Scripture is just full of cute stories. And people don't believe them because they've had some bad experience with religion that's turned them off to the word of God.

Well, trust me; Exodus is a history book, and Moses is just as real a person as Honest Abe. And in that history book, Moses says, "I want to see you, God."

"You can't see me and live, Moses," God says. "But let me tell you who I am."

He doesn't say, "Hey Moses, check out that star. Isn't that cool? That was me, bro. And see the sky all around it? I was thinking blue or yellow, and I went with blue. What do you think?"

He doesn't say anything like that. He says, "Let me tell you who I am. I am the Lord your God. I am Yahweh." That's a Hebrew word we don't have a very good translation for in English, but it essentially means "the self-existent one." Back then you couldn't even utter the word, because it was that powerful.

But God could say the Hebrew word, of course, because He was God. "I am the creator," He said to Moses. "I am everything. I am compassionate. I am gracious. I am merciful. I am patient. And I forgive iniquity. I forgive sin. I forgive."

Out of all the things God could have chosen to say about Himself, the first thing out of God's mouth was, "I am compassionate, merciful, and forgiving." Why aren't we speaking that all the time? That's the message we should be running around planet Earth with, the message we should have ready every moment—the message that should be pouring out of us in our words and actions. Nothing else.

You're probably familiar with the term "Bible thumpers"—Christians who metaphorically "thump" other people with their thick, black Bibles and tell them how to live. What a horrible way to share God's message of love and forgiveness. We don't need some behavior modification manual. There should be no thumping, only love.

The goal is not to get people to change their behavior. I'm never going to run around trying to get homosexuals to stop being homosexuals, or men and women who are living together before marriage to move out. That's not what this is about! It's about who God is—and then, because of His wonderful love and compassion, who we are in Him. God is able to change behavior.

We need to introduce people to the compassionate, loving, merciful God. As they see Him and know

Him—as they become intimate with God—*that's* when the change happens.

But it may not always happen. Maybe they won't change; maybe they will. Our business is to introduce them to the God of the universe and let the Holy Spirit do His work in their life. Jesus said to his disciples to wait for the promise of the Father. The promise was the Holy Spirit, that is where the power is.

So who are *you*?

If you're a child of God, then you have an answer to that question. And if you're not, I can promise you that question gets a whole lot more fun to answer once you are.

So right now, do you feel good about yourself because you are in a relationship with God, or because you believe you are doing everything right, or both?

39

YOU'RE FREE TO FAIL

You've heard of Abraham, right? The great patriarch, Father of Israel, et cetera. A man so loyal to God, he was ready to sacrifice his own son until He spared the boy's life in the eleventh hour.

But did you know that Abraham came from a family of devil worshippers? That his parents made idols for a living? The guy didn't exactly have a sparkling pedigree, yet God chose him anyway. And Abe responded to the call. But the thing is, it could've been anybody.

I use this story to illustrate that there is nothing inherently good in man for God to choose him. We are all flawed and unmistakably broken. But God *does* choose us, giving us His forgiveness, His grace, and His mercy. He chooses us because of *His* character, not ours.

Every week I get together with a group of men to

talk about the Scriptures. Lately we've been talking about God's grace. We talk about how God freely gives us forgiveness, not based on anything we've done, but based on who He is. In other words, there's nothing in humankind that would cause God to move toward us on our own merits. He's not sitting up in heaven going, "Oh my goodness, did you see what Mike Moore just did? What a great guy. I've got to go down there and reward him immediately. I didn't think he was that good, but boy, did he surprise me!" That's not how it works.

So last week, one of the guys in the group said, "Stop right there, Mike. You keep talking about the grace of God this, the grace of God that. Are you telling me that I can do anything I want to because God's already forgiven me?"

"Great question," I said. "That leads us to another question: what is it you want to do?"

He looked at me sideways. "What do you mean?"

I shrugged. "You're asking if God's grace means you can do anything. So what do you want to do?"

The guy shifted in his seat. I could tell he didn't like my line of questioning. "I don't know," he said. "All I'm saying is, you talk about this whole grace of God thing, and how we're free to live our lives, and that we can do anything we want because God's already forgiven us."

I wouldn't let up on him. "Which still begs the question, what do you want to do?"

He sighed. "Let's say I wanted to go have an affair on my wife."

"Now we're getting somewhere," I said. "By the way, guys, I want you to know this is a safe space, so let's get completely real with each other." I turned back around to face this guy. "So, is that what you want to do?"

"No, no," he said, backpedaling fast. "I'm just saying, if we're free, doesn't it mean I can do whatever I want to do?"

"You didn't answer my question," I said. "Do you want to have an affair?"

"No, I don't!" he practically shouted.

"Okay," I said. "Why not?"

And his answer showed me where he stood. He looked right at me and said, "Because the word of God says I can't."

"Bingo," I said. This guy had just hit the nail on the head, whether he knew it or not.

I turned to the rest of the group. "You're all worried about God's grace and God's forgiveness, so you are putting yourself under a bunch of rules and regulations. You're telling me the only thing keeping you from having an affair is that there's a rule that says you can't? That's not God's grace. That's God's anger and punishment. You're afraid of being punished.

"I challenge you to go tell your wife exactly that. Matter of fact, I'll pay for it. I'll give you a five hundred dollar voucher so you can go to a real fancy restaurant, get a great bottle of wine, sit down for a romantic dinner, and even treat her to a fancy hotel room that night. Have your bride put on her best cocktail dress, and as you're staring into her eyes over your candle-light dinner, about to cut into that juicy steak, I want you to lean over and say, 'Baby, the only reason I'm not having an affair is because there's a rule in the word of God that says I can't.' See how far you get."

When we talk about the freedom of God's grace, people so often boil it down to, "What can I get away with?" That man was not alone; I can't tell you how many men *and* women say to me, "So you're saying we're free to sin."

What I'm saying is you are free to make a choice.

"Listen to what I'm saying," I said to the guys in our group. "It should never be, 'I want to have an affair on my wife, but I can't.' Are you free to? Yes, you are free to choose! But why would you? If you love your wife, why would you have sex with that woman over there, knowing she is going to be some other man's wife in the future? Why would you steal from that woman and her future husband? Why would you steal from your own wife?"

God's grace has forgiven us—past, present, and future—for everything we've ever done to break "the rules." Why? So we can be free to finally choose God, choose love, and put other people and their needs ahead of our own. We aren't free to do that when we're in bondage to some archaic rule. You are only free to do the right thing when you're free to also do the *wrong* thing. The choice is yours.

The freedom to choose Him when before we were set free by the finished, completed work that Jesus Christ accomplished for us at the cross? That freedom didn't exist. You had to obey. Now you get to!

Let's try the following thought exercise.

Let's say you're free to do anything you want, anything at all, with zero consequences. You won't go to jail. You won't get hurt. You won't die.

What would you do?

If you've got an index card lying around, grab it. A piece of paper works just as well. Write down exactly what you'd do. It's just between you and God.

What's in your heart? Would you go kill somebody? Cheat on your wife? Drive to a strip club? Steal money out of a bank? What would you do, if you could do anything? Write out the whole list.

Now look at that piece of paper. That list is what's in your heart. So my question for you is, "What's keeping you from doing it?"

Maybe you have noble reasons. Maybe you don't cheat on your wife because it would hurt your wife, and you love her too much to hurt her like that. If that's the case, take that one off the list.

But if your reasons include stuff like, "What would my wife think if I had an affair?" "What would my church think if I stole money?" "I could never do that; I'd be too afraid of getting caught," then that stuff stays on the list. I want to know every single thing you'd do if not for the voices going, "The Bible says I can't. I'd get in trouble. What would my friends think? Wouldn't that damage my good name?"

If that's why you're not doing the stuff on your list, you have to leave those reasons behind, because they have nothing to do with love or grace.

I'm not going to make you burn your list or rip it up into tiny pieces. The stuff on the list is what's in your heart. Start being honest with yourself about what you want, because only then can you understand what it means to be free, and only once you are free can you accept the gift of God's love.

I have a friend who has an organization called "family"—Forgetting About Me I Love You. Is it possible to forget about yourself for three days, or even a day for that matter? Or maybe an hour?

40

WHAT WOULD ROBERTA SAY?

A friend asked me to do a funeral for one of her friends. The late woman's name was Roberta, and she was forty-eight years old.

My friend had come to some of my events and heard me speak. "I'd really like you to come and give a message of hope to these people," she said.

"I'd love to," I told her. I went and stood in front of a church full of people to eulogize Roberta and talk about her life.

I didn't know Roberta, and I didn't recognize a single face in the crowd. When I stood up, here's the thing I communicated to the group: "We don't need more answers to life's questions. What we need is more hope. All I have to say about Roberta is what everybody has told me about her. And wow—what an amazing woman."

Inside, my thoughts were very different. I had all these questions. Why did Roberta die at forty-eight? Why did she get this illness? Why did this happen?

But here's the thing; Roberta doesn't have those questions anymore. Dead people don't have questions; they're not looking for answers. And we—the living—don't need answers, either. We need more hope in our lives.

"If Roberta could stand up, walk out of this casket, and sit down in front of us and talk," I said, "here's what I think she would say.

"'Put your life on pause for a moment and ask yourself this question: where is the hope? Where is *your* hope? What is your hope in? Because if our hope is not in the One who made us and filled us with Himself, then I'm not sure we're in the right hope. What are we hoping for? Are we hoping in the God of the universe, because He's got all the answers? Or is our hope in something else?

"There are a lot of gods on planet Earth—the different gods we all carry around with us—so let me introduce you to the God I'm talking about. I'm talking about a God who sent His one and only Son, and that Son walked on the planet, was crucified, died, and was buried, only to be resurrected again so He could sit at the right hand of the Father, and fill us with his Spirit.

"That's the God I'm talking about. The God of

Abraham, Isaac, and Jacob—and the God of Jesus of Nazareth. There are a lot of gods, but that's the God I'm talking about. Not a God of rules and regulations. Not a God of behavior modification.

"My God says, 'I want you to learn to see the way I'm seeing. Not through your résumé, not through your failures, but through what I've done for you. I want you to receive my love—take all of it, and don't ask for answers. Just look at me for the hope that you need to walk around on planet Earth, and share that with the world around you.'"

So I said to Roberta's grieving friends and family, "What if Roberta were sitting up here beside me and she said, 'Put your life on pause for a moment.' And what if we actually did that, and we stopped? Just for a moment, what if we let go of all the things around us—all the circumstances, the minutiae that distract us, the thoughts and feelings and actions? What would happen if we could stop and go, 'Okay, why am I here? What is my purpose for being alive on planet Earth? What is it I'm alive for?'"

None of us remembers being born. It wasn't my decision to be alive, and I don't know when I'm going to die. It wasn't even my mother and father's decision. It was God's decision to give me life and bring me into the world.

And if that's true—if I'm God's answer, God's

thought, God's decision—then the Manufacturer of the human race must have a purpose for me. He's the reason I am alive, and nothing is by accident. If all that is true, then I need to pause and go, "What is the hope I carry around, and what is my purpose on planet Earth?"

That's what Roberta gave us that day. A chance to pause and reflect and ask, "What am I doing here? What is God's purpose for me and my life?"

41

OLD BONE OR FRESH STEAK?

They say you can't teach an old dog new tricks, but I did once.

My neighbor Jack had a beautiful black lab, Bernie, who was the friendliest dog I'd ever met. Black dogs at shelters have the hardest time getting adopted. People think they're scary, that they look mean. But Bernie was as sweet as pie, even though he was bigger than a wolf. Some of the kids on the street got nervous when they saw him, but Bernie just ran up to them and wanted to play.

Jack knew I loved Bernie, so he brought him to my house whenever he stopped by. And every time I saw Bernie, he was chewing on the same old bone. Now, this wasn't a new bone. He had been chewing on it for years. Years! There was no juice left in it; it was dry as a ... well, as a bone. It was also disgusting, completely filthy from years of accumulated dirt and slobber. But no matter how hard I tried to wrench it from his jaws, Bernie refused to let go.

That didn't stop me from trying. One day I said, "Come here, Bernie," and I wrestled with him for several minutes, trying to get him to let go of that bone.

"There's no way he's letting that bone go," Jack said.

"No way, huh?"

Jack had thrown down the gauntlet, and there's nothing I love more than a good challenge. I'd spent years working with people, helping men and women "let go" of the stuff that was holding them back. Shouldn't I be able to use the same techniques on a four-legged animal?

"I bet I can get that bone out of your dog's mouth," I told Jack. "Maybe not today, maybe not tomorrow, but I'll do it."

He grinned. "Sure you will, Mike."

Months went by, and I forgot about the challenge until one afternoon when I had a few people over for a barbecue. My guests were all gnawing on the juicy bone-in New York strip steak I had grilled for them when I saw Jack walking by with Bernie.

"Why don't you come on over!" I called to Jack.

"Can't. My wife's cooking dinner."

"Just for a minute. We've got so much extra food."

I caught Jack sniffing the air, no doubt smelling those luscious New York strips, and—like his dog—he couldn't resist a good bone-in. He and Bernie walked into my yard.

As usual, Bernie was chomping on that same old bone. I tried grabbing it from his mouth like I always did. No success.

While I was preparing a plate of steak for Jack, I had an idea.

I walked towards Jack, holding a succulent piece of meat with tons of fat on it. I could tell Jack was happy he had decided to come by. When he extended his hand to take the plate, I threw him for a loop.

I kneeled down and put it in front of Bernie!

"You said you weren't hungry, but I bet your boy is," I said to Jack.

Bernie came up to the meat and sniffed it. Not two seconds later, he dropped his bone and began to chow down on the meat. He attacked that steak like he'd never ingested a morsel of food in his life; he wagged his tail and sucked up every last bite. In the meantime, I yanked his old bone away and ran to throw it in the trash before Bernie noticed it was missing.

Jack was grinning from ear to ear. "Well I have to give it to you, Mike. I didn't think it was possible."

"Your dog's smarter than you thought," I told him, before returning to the grill to fix Jack a piece of steak.

I didn't want him to be envious of the dog!

Why did Bernie suddenly drop his bone when he'd been so adamantly against it for years? Because he had enough sense to see that there was more value in the fresh New York strip steak than in his old bone. It looked better, it was juicier, and it tasted a heck of a lot better than that dirty old thing.

People aren't so different from dogs. Sometimes we hold onto our old beliefs and our old dogmas (pun intended) until we realize there are better alternatives. It's only then that we begin to let go.

We all have the power to be like Bernie and reevaluate whether our ideas are actually good, or if they just feel comfortable and familiar. When we see that there's a fresh juicy steak out there waiting to be eaten, and there's no room to taste it because our mouth's full of old bone, the decision becomes a lot easier.

The old bone that we won't let go of is a relic from our past—ideas our parents or churches taught us, ideas that have become dry and flavorless as we've evolved beyond them. By challenging ourselves to learn new tricks and let go of the bones that are holding us back, we can avoid the trap of becoming old dogs.

And you know what Bernie got at the end of the lesson? A brand *new* bone to chomp on!

What bone do you need to let go of?

42

TURNIPS FOR DEAD PEOPLE

When was the last time you got real with your-self about a belief or bias you have that is just plain wrong? It takes a lot of courage to challenge a long-held opinion—especially if you've invested years in telling yourself you are 100 percent right.

When push comes to shove, we're all sticks-in-the-mud, every last one of us. Being averse to change is in our nature. We cling to our beliefs and perceptions—even our *mis*conceptions—as if life depends on it, when in reality, it's sometimes the other way around. Our life depends on us breaking out of the old way of thinking.

Take, for example, my relationship with turnips.

It all started with Aunt Violet. When I was a kid, my parents used to take weekend getaways and leave my older brother and me with my mother's cousin. Aunt

Violet was an olive-skinned Italian lady with big circles under her eyes and cold, clammy hands. She lived in a ramshackle Victorian house with dark velvet drapes that were always closed. Every night, she played Chopin on her out-of-tune grand piano in the dimly lit parlor. There was something very Gothic about Aunt Violet.

"Pack your bags, you're going to Aunt Violet's," my mother would say as she dragged my brother and me from our hiding spot in the basement.

"No!" my brother would cry. "She's scary."

"He's right, Mom," I chimed in. "She smells like dead people."

"How can you even say that? She's family. You don't say those things about family."

The problem was it was *true*. Aunt Violet worked at the neighborhood funeral home. Plus, her house was filled with dying flora. Every room was overflowing with lavish bouquets of three-day-old flowers. Everywhere my brother and I turned, we were struck with the cloying smell of death.

We were also confused. Aunt Violet never seemed to have a boyfriend—which didn't surprise us in the slightest—yet she always had these bouquets all over the place. Who the heck was bringing her flowers?

One day, my brother dared me to open one of the cards attached to the bouquet. "We love you, Big Al," was inscribed in big, black print.

At dinner that night, I got up the nerve to ask Aunt Violet, "Who's Big Al?"

She shrugged. "From what I hear, he was a plumber. And a very nice man."

That's when I realized Aunt Violet filled the house with leftover flowers from her job at the funeral home. *She stole dead people's flowers.* If you can think of something creepier to an eight-year-old boy, I'd love to hear it.

My brother and I looked at each other in horror as Aunt Violet reached for the turnips. She always had turnips, at every meal. Of course, by then, we'd completely lost our appetite. What if she was serving us dead people's turnips, too?

"No more turnips for me, please," I peeped.

She didn't listen. Instead she ladled out another helping of turnips. There were no alternative meal options. It was either turnips or we'd go to bed hungry.

Fast-forward about fifteen years. I was in college, waiting in line at the cafeteria in the athletic dorm. The athletes got to wait in a special line and had unlimited access to food. We had first dibs on the meat because we needed to eat more protein than the average college student.

I knew all the names of the people who worked in the dining hall because I wanted to know who to ask for my extra food. I still remember Margaret. She was a real sweetheart, always reminding us to change our clocks for daylight saving time. One day, she said, "Michael, give me your plate. I've got some turnips here."

"Margaret," I said. "do not put turnips on that plate. Don't even think about it. I'm an adult and I don't eat turnips."

"Why? What's wrong with turnips?" she asked.

"I just don't like them."

I didn't tell her the real reason—that turnips brought back bad memories. They reminded me of feeling abandoned by my parents when they left us with Aunt Violet. They reminded me of death. They reminded me of my own mortality.

Fast-forward about twenty *more* years, to a brightly lit doctor's office. I was at a routine physical after turning forty, and my doctor was telling me about foods with antioxidants in them. "You know, Mike," he said, "one of the foods that greatly helps reduce the risk of colon cancer is turnips. You should consider adding them to your diet."

I sat up a little straighter. "You're kidding me!"

I had spent my entire adulthood proudly avoiding turnips because of my bad association with them. But when I found out about their health benefits, everything changed. As a full-grown man, I was able to think logically rather than emotionally about turnips. I knew I didn't want to get colon cancer, so I was able to make a new association with my dreaded enemy. Instead of connecting them with the stench of funerals and my painful memories, I began to see them through the filter of good health.

I started to see other things differently, too. As an adult reflecting on my childhood, I saw my parents' actions in a new light. They weren't abandoning us as a punishment; they were taking time to work on their marriage, spending precious time together *without* the stress of kids. In leaving us with Aunt Violet, they were teaching us to be flexible, to learn acceptance that we couldn't always get what we wanted, and sometimes we had to eat turnips, or else starve.

And in making this new association, I was able to see Aunt Violet differently. She wasn't feeding us turnips as a form of torture, but because she recognized their nutritional value. Or maybe she just really liked them. All I know is that I feel a little silly now, remembering myself as a scared kid, thinking everything in that house somehow had dead people smell on it. I'm glad I'm not that kid anymore.

Are you someone who refuses to grow—someone who can't change and evolve? Do you refuse to admit when you were wrong? Are you stuck in the same old hell of ignorant existence? If you're living like that, you're just going through the motions. You're not alive—you're living life as a dead person.

But if you learn to love turnips—or whatever the "turnips" are in your life, the things that scare you or hold you back—then you're back in the land of the living.

Welcome back!

Are there any "turnips" that you aren't eating today?

43

"PLEASE ALLOW ME TO GROW"

You're walking through a beautiful park, one of the oldest parks in your neighborhood. You love this park. Your parents used to take you to play here when you were a kid, and you took your kids to play here, and you hope someday your kids will take their kids to play here, too.

But as you walk past the duck pond and the little playground, you notice a new sign. It says, in big bold print, **"STOP. DO NOT WALK ON GRASS."**

How do you feel? You might be a little insulted by this sign telling you what to do. It could have at least been worded less aggressively, you think. Wouldn't "Please keep off the grass" have sufficed? It's such a strong admonition, you wonder what it would cost if you *did* walk on the grass. Would a policemen spring out from behind a tree and write you a ticket? Would the head of the neighborhood association suddenly appear and give you a stern talking to?

If you're like me, when you see that sign, the very first thing you want to do is walk on that grass. Maybe you didn't even want to before—but as soon as someone tells you that you can't do something, you're dying to do it!

So imagine the sign didn't say that at all. Imagine it said, **"PLEASE ALLOW ME TO GROW."**

Now, as soon as I see that sign, I have a very different reaction. I'm going to think, "Wow, I don't want to hurt the grass! I'll be very careful not to step on it."

Two very different messages are both trying to achieve the same goal: to keep me off the grass. The first one makes me feel defensive and angry, like I *want* to step on the grass, just to prove I can. The second makes me feel thoughtful and loving, like I want to make it my personal responsibility to protect that grass so it can grow into soft green blades that my children's children will play in someday.

It's all a matter of perspective—which is a fancy word for the way we interpret the stuff in our world. Reading the first sign, we feel condemned. Reading the second sign, we feel free—and far more likely to choose the right course of action.

The concept of freedom is hard for the human mind to grasp. We so often interpret freedom as "the right to go out and do whatever I want." Every time people say this to me, I want to shake them by the shoulders and say, "Why do you always go to that side of it? Why can't you say, 'I'm finally free to love somebody! To do work I'm passionate about! To serve my community! To set a positive example for my friends and family!'" Instead of life being about what you *have* to do, why not revel in the things you *get* to do, now that you're free?

There are churches all over the world that teach behavior modification. "You've got a problem with pornography?" they ask. "Don't worry; we'll get you to the right men's group. We'll put a special blocking software program on your computer." Really? You're going to put software on a guy's computer and assume that keeps him from porn? There's a flaw at the root of that thinking. Even if the guy *does* curtail his porn addiction, he's doing it for fear of man, not for the love of God. And not for the love of his wife because he doesn't want to destroy his marriage with that garbage going into his heart, soul, and mind.

We have to constantly ask ourselves, "Am I doing what I'm doing for the love of God or the fear of punishment?" The end results are very different: one is life, and one is death.

Obviously, there are consequences to the choices we make on this earth. I'm free to choose my behavior, or I'm free to choose my consequences, but I can't choose both. If my choice is to not go to jail, then that free choice to kill somebody is taken away from me. If I don't want to go to jail, I can't kill somebody.

Conversely, if I want to kill somebody, then I can't choose not to go to jail. That choice is taken away from me. So I get to choose my behavior or my consequences. I can't choose both. But whatever choice I make is entirely up to me.

God says to all of us, "You're free to do that. I give you that freedom as my child. But my love will never leave you. I won't change my mind about you."

When God punished the sins of the world by sending His only son to die on the cross, I wasn't around yet—which means all my behavior was taken care of 2,000 years ago, two millennia before I was born! He already knew my entire future, every mistake and bad choice I would ever make. And if that's true, then the things I am going to do five years from now have already been forgiven before I do them.

Knowing that doesn't make me feel like I can do whatever and get away with it. On the contrary, it makes me want to live right! But I also know I'm going to make mistakes. And if I spend my whole life trying not to mess up, I'm focused on the wrong thing.

I should be focused on the people in front of me. How can I love them? How do I get out of myself and be humble enough to see the passion in other people and help them realize their dreams? How can I allow them to grow?

We've all felt the sting of condemnation. We feel condemned by people outside the church and sometimes even by our brothers and sisters in Christ. But for those of us who have put our faith in Jesus, God has declared "no condemnation." I am unaccusable. So when I start self-condemning, I spiral. I keep going down and down and down and down. I keep doing the things that I don't want to do. The very thing that keeps me in bondage when I condemn myself only strengthens its grip on my life, forging thicker and thicker chains.

Paradoxically, if I know I am free to do something and that I will not be condemned, even if I make that choice, I won't do it. It's like seeing that "Please Allow Me to Grow" sign. Because I've been given the freedom to make my own choice, I'll choose not to walk on the grass. And in so doing, I'll choose another, better path.

Take a moment and think of three things that are negative and turn them into a positive. For example, "Don't be late," versus "Other people's time is very important." Or "Don't steal" versus "Someone worked hard to earn money and buy this product."

Can you think of three?

Final Thoughts

THE HEART BEHIND THE INSTRUCTION

Most of us grew up hearing: "Don't do this, don't do that." As rebellious kids and teenagers, all we wanted to do was to break the rules.

But if we knew the heart behind the instruction, we might have felt differently. That's the thing we're looking for in a relationship with God. A Jew will look at the Torah and go, "This is the heart of a loving father," whereas a Gentile like me will look at the scriptures and go, "I'm not going to do that. It's just another rule. I'm done following rules."

But there's a heart behind the instruction. Very few people get to see that heart, but it's there. If we saw the heart behind the instruction, we'd go, "Oh, yeah, I'm happy to do that." We'd understand that it's in our best interest—and that God is on our side.

Imagine a gentleman and his wife, a proper British

couple, who have just boarded a train in London. They're dressed nicely, maybe going away for the weekend. The train is about to take off when along comes a disheveled woman. She's an awful sight. She has dirt and mud all over her—clearly hasn't bathed in weeks—and she is cradling a small baby to her chest. The baby is just as dirty as the woman, caked in filth and grime so thick that the couple can hardly see his face.

"Honey," says the lady to her husband, "we have to take care of them."

The man watches the sad pair through the train window and knows his wife is right. What does this man believe? He believes this woman is a homeless person with a baby, and that they need his help. What does that belief cause? Compassion. And what does that compassion cause him to do? Open up his wallet.

He's about to stick a hundred pounds sterling through the train window when the conductor grabs his arm. "Don't give anything to her," the conductor says.

The man is angry. "I can't believe you're keeping me from helping this woman! She's clearly poor and destitute. How could you be so callous?" He says some choice words, because now his belief is causing him anger, and that anger is causing him to say things he probably shouldn't.

"You don't understand," the conductor says. "She's a fake. She does this for a living. The baby is on rent, and she does this at other stations."

Instantly, the man's belief changes. He thinks to himself, "Oh my goodness, she's a fake." His new belief causes him a new feeling. Now he's angry with the woman. He feels like she tried to take advantage of him. Frankly, he's even a little angry with his wife for falling for the woman's act and dragging him into it.

The British gentleman opens his wallet and stuffs the two fifty-pound notes back inside, hoping no one saw him be so trusting, so naïve.

How did that exchange start? With a belief, followed by another belief, followed by another. The man's beliefs changed in seconds. And when his belief about the situation changed, it caused a change in behavior. At each point he received different information, new facts that caused him to change the way he behaved.

Remember, we look for what we believe. What we look for, we find. And when what we find causes a certain feeling, it causes a behavior.

What would it be like if we put this lesson to use in our lives—if we realized that our beliefs cause our behaviors, and that our beliefs may very well be wrong?

Let's say you are driving on a street near your

house and a car cuts you off. The driver very nearly clips the side of your car, an action that makes you furious. You want to tailgate him, flip him the bird, and yell nasty names. But you don't have all the facts, do you? Maybe the person who cut you off is desperately trying to get to the hospital with a sick child. Maybe he just lost a loved one.

I have a friend who was driving with his young daughter, and the guy behind him was swerving like crazy, almost ramming into the back of my friend's car. My friend was outraged and started cursing at this crazy driver, until his little girl looked over at him and said, "Daddy, what if he lost his wife and he's trying to get to the hospital?"

What an amazing thing to say. Where did that come from? How did a seven-year-old child get to that place of compassion and love? She certainly didn't have all the facts or information, but her behavior started with what she believed.

Every decision we make in life is an emotional decision—every single decision. Even if you think and overthink it, it's still an emotional decision. It may start in our mind, but our mind is just a computer calculating what's in our hearts, the center of our life. Our heart is where our beliefs are deeply ingrained, whether it's the stuff we learned as kids or the stuff we've adopted as we've grown up. For most of us, it's a combination of the two.

If you want to change your behavior, you have to change what you believe. That's where it all starts. And if you want to change what you believe, start with God.

When we look at God's book of promises, we have a choice to believe or not believe. And if we say, "I believe this," those thoughts become ideas in our mind, and those ideas become dreams when we absorb them all the way through our being. That's when they get inside our hearts.

It doesn't come out of a sense of obligation. It's not, "I have to do this" or "I have to do that because God said to." It's more like osmosis. God's words and thoughts and promises saturate our whole being— they become *who we are*. And once God's Word gets inside of us, it manifests into reality. We can't help but walk out God's truths from the inside.

All of us are guilty of saying one thing and doing the opposite. We may know the right thing to do, but somewhere in our hearts, we are believing something that's causing us to act differently. That's when we know it is time to change our belief system.

We cannot change other people. We are only responsible for ourselves. When we believe what Christ did at the cross for the forgiveness of our sins, he sends us a helper, the Holy Spirit. He's the one that empowers us to believe everything that God says in his Word concerning our identity and our acceptance with God. Are your feelings consistent with what God says about you?